The Man Who Drove With His Eyes Closed

Also by The Barefoot Doctor

BAREFOOT DOCTOR'S GUIDE TO THE TAO:
A Spiritual Handbook for the Urban Warrior

BAREFOOT DOCTOR'S HANDBOOK FOR HEROES:
A Spiritual Guide to Fame & Fortune

BAREFOOT DOCTOR'S HANDBOOK FOR MODERN LOVERS:
A Spiritual Guide to Truly Amazing Love and Sex

BAREFOOT DOCTOR'S HANDBOOK FOR THE URBAN WARRIOR:
A Spiritual Survival Guide

DEAR BAREFOOT: *Taoist Wisdom for Everyday Living*

INSTANT ENLIGHTENMENT: *108 Blessings*

THE INVINCIBILITY TRAINING: *Total Transformation in 3 Days*

LIBERATION: *The Perfect Holistic Antidote to Stress,
Depression and Other Unhealthy States of Mind*

MANIFESTO: *The Internal Revolution*

PURE: *A Path to Peace, Power and Prosperity*

RETURN OF THE URBAN WARRIOR:
High-Speed Spirituality for People on the Run

TWISTED FABLES FOR TWISTED MINDS:
This Will Either Heal You or Make You Insane

Please visit Hay House UK: **www.hayhouse.co.uk;** Hay House USA: **www.hayhouse.com®;** Hay House Australia: **www.hayhouse.com.au;** Hay House South Africa: **www.hayhouse.co.za;** Hay House India: **www.hayhouse.co.in**

The Man Who Drove With His Eyes Closed

Stephen Russell
(The Barefoot Doctor)

HAY HOUSE

Australia • Canada • Hong Kong • India
South Africa • United Kingdom • United States

First published and distributed in the United Kingdom by:
Hay House UK Ltd, 292B Kensal Rd, London W10 5BE. Tel.: (44) 20 8962 1230;
Fax: (44) 20 8962 1239. www.hayhouse.co.uk

Published and distributed in the United States of America by:
Hay House, Inc., PO Box 5100, Carlsbad, CA 92018-5100. Tel.: (1) 760 431 7695 or
(800) 654 5126; Fax: (1) 760 431 6948 or (800) 650 5115. www.hayhouse.com

Published and distributed in Australia by:
Hay House Australia Ltd, 18/36 Ralph St, Alexandria NSW 2015.
Tel.: (61) 2 9669 4299; Fax: (61) 2 9669 4144. www.hayhouse.com.au

Published and distributed in the Republic of South Africa by:
Hay House SA (Pty), Ltd, PO Box 990, Witkoppen 2068. Tel./Fax: (27) 11 467 8904.
www.hayhouse.co.za

Published and distributed in India by:
Hay House Publishers India, Muskaan Complex, Plot No.3, B-2, Vasant Kunj, New
Delhi – 110 070. Tel.: (91) 11 4176 1620; Fax: (91) 11 4176 1630.
www.hayhouse.co.in

Distributed in Canada by:
Raincoast, 9050 Shaughnessy St, Vancouver, BC V6P 6E5. Tel.: (1) 604 323 7100;
Fax: (1) 604 323 2600

© Stephen Russell, the Barefoot Doctor, 2009

Editorial supervision: Jill Kramer • Design: Amanda Armour

The moral rights of the author have been asserted.

A catalogue record for this book is available from the British Library.

ISBN 978-1-84850-143-0

Printed and bound in Great Britain by CPI Bookmarque, Croydon, CR0 4TD.

To all my teachers.

And special thanks to my dear friend and brother on the path, Danny Buckler, who encouraged me to write this book.

Contents

Foreword

I'll be frank. There's something I don't get. I'm just back from a two-day trip to Legoland with the family, where we must have spent about £500 altogether. £500 on burgers and chips, entry into a series of long queues, bits of coloured plastic arranged into various shapes. Don't get me wrong: I loved the experience. But I now sit with this tome in my hands, retailing at £8.99.

£8.99 is what they were charging for a mug with the photo of your screaming family dropping from the top of the rollercoaster.

£8.99 is what it cost to order a club sandwich in the hotel once we got back with our collection of family-plastered mugs.

And here I am, now, holding a text with a retail price of £8.99 that contains more wisdom (and transmitted in such an entertaining manner) than I've come across in a long time.

I just don't get it.

But this question of 'value' is interesting, and pertinent to this great book. Barefoot recounts his experiences with so many powerful teachers, in an era long before you could do yoga in your local gym, tai chi in the church hall or find alternative health advice on the shelves of WH Smith. It was an era when you had to go in search of knowledge beyond your high street. You can feel the pioneer spirit of Barefoot and his teachers on every page of this book: people on the very edge of learning about themselves and their place in the universe. It's clear that if you manage to find the one person in the land who can teach you the internal martial of Hsing I, then you're going to value that knowledge and regard it as the gold that it is.

And Barefoot came across lots of 'gold' on his journey to becoming the Barefoot Doctor in 1989. The stories are fascinating. But I expected that. Barefoot is such a good storyteller, and such a generous and perceptive observer of people that I knew I'd be entertained. What I didn't expect was that he would unpack his slowly accumulated knowledge so thoroughly and effectively.

The effect is a book that looks, on the face of it, like an autobiography (or, rather, multi-biography) but presents wisdoms of every colour on every page. Through this format, Barefoot seems to have deconstructed his own guru wisdom in a way that is both uniquely accessible and entertaining.

And it seems to me an act of great generosity to download this accumulated wisdom in such a way.

Especially at £8.99 a copy.

So back to this value point.

It's tempting to long for the pioneer days once more: when the supply of knowledge was limited and relatively inaccessible, when you had to fight for what you learned and treated the resultant knowledge with respect and 'valued' it highly.

But I for one am happy to live now in an age of instantly accessible wisdom: when you can access 1,000 gurus from your own desk or armchair. The trick now is to select the real wisdom and to give it the value it deserves. This is no easy matter.

Peculiarly, this over-supply in the wisdom market makes it as hard to find the gold as it was before.

And, in this context, we can still be pioneers: making our own personal way through the sea of mystery, trying to locate the bits that ring true for us.

Personally, when it comes to wisdom available in text format, I read a huge amount, then settle on just a few works, by a few authors. And I give them the highest value. I read them again and again, taking in every word until those words are part of me.

I've done that with the work of Barefoot over the years. His work is gold.

And this work is the shiniest, most exquisite example of gold you'll find.

Thank your lucky stars that its monetary value is a mere £8.99 and treat it like the gold it is . . . treasure it, and let its power and beauty begin to adorn your life.

John C. Parkin, author of
F**k It: The Ultimate Spiritual Way
and The Way of F**k It.

Introduction

I'm a supercharged Taoist.

And that's a crazy way to start a book.

I do so because no doubt I'm partly crazy but also to grab your attention. I have a story to tell, and I believe it could be inspiring for you. I tend to suffer from compulsive liberationist tendencies – in other words, I'm a natural-born liberator – so I hope reading this book serves to set you free of anything holding you back from transforming your own life into the most magnificent adventure imaginable.

I say I'm a supercharged Taoist because for more than 35 years I've been training in Taoist martial arts, chi gung, and meditation. Just as it promised in the instruction leaflets, these practices have generated an accumulation of supercharged energy that courses through me and everything I do. This makes my life exciting, endlessly varied, and full of adventure. Using the ancient Taoist *wu-wei* manifesting methods – focusing on being, not doing, and intending things into existence rather than trying to force them – I'm able to create reality as I wish it to be, almost instantaneously. I say this humbly. Also, by letting the Taoist philosophy underscore everything

I think, do, and say, I've learned to be flexible in my thinking. Flexibility lets me enjoy all aspects of the ride to the fullest, whether in an up phase or a down one. I feel blessed by all this and want to share my good fortune with you. I want you, in your own style, to be blessed in the same way.

I've always had a desire to share the wonder of the Tao with others. That's been my motivation for as long as I can remember. I have an enthusiasm for it, a childlike exuberance that carries me through life in a way that uplifts and cheers me. I've found that over the years my exuberance has helped others feel exuberant too. That is how I want this book to leave you feeling, and I want all of Britain and the whole world beyond to feel exuberant too.

In order to paint a clear picture of what I do, I'm never really sure where to start, so I'll start here for now and see how it goes: I'm a writer (which is how the two of us got into this pickle in the first place). I'm a communicator. I'm a healer. I'm a public speaker. I'm a martial arts and meditation teacher. I'm a coach. I'm a workshop leader. I'm a philosopher. I'm a broadcaster. I'm a music producer. I'm a DJ. I'm a website content provider. I make TV programmes. I'm even a perfumer.

Physically speaking, though, I spend a lot of time interacting with circuitry and chips, tapping my fingertips onto small squares of sprung plastic on a keyboard – up and down and a bit to the side for hours and hours almost every day. When not doing that, I'm sometimes pressing smaller plastic squares and talking into other bits of plastic. When not doing that, I'm rhythmically pressing, plucking or strumming steel strings; tickling the ivories; or slapping drum skins. When not doing *that,* I stretch and flex my vocal chords to make sound come out of my mouth into microphones on stands. Amid this tapping, plucking, tickling and all, I move my person and various bits of clothing through time and space and keep myself clean, fresh and nourished; and can regularly be found waving my arms in the air slowly or fast. Often when I'm doing much of this, I'm walking or sitting – sometimes with my eyes closed – on floors or in chairs of various descriptions, and in a multitude of diverse settings: in the air, on the ocean waves, but mostly on dry land. And generally there are lots of other people involved in what I'm doing, directly or indirectly.

Existentially speaking, I'm constantly exploring new, creative and innovative ways of transmitting not just the message of the Tao, but the love that informs it, to as many people as possible. And while I'm doing it, I have as much fun, with as much human warmth and colour included, with as many people as I can.

My desire is to encourage the whole world to relax a few degrees more. I believe this simple alteration is all that's required to enable us to communicate more freely, honestly and intelligently with each other; and in that communication find the way to live in peace and plenty on this glorious planet of ours for many generations to come.

It seems clear enough to me that when we humans (all the way from grass roots to leadership level) are more relaxed, we tend to rise less quickly to anger and are more willing to talk sense with one another. We're more likely to negotiate from a place of fairness rather than one of greed, and to honor each other's differences rather than use them as cause for suspicion. It seems blatantly clear to me that the more we relax, the more lubricated the wheels of our global society will be, and so peace and plenty will be facilitated by and for all of us.

As we all can see, the need for this is becoming increasingly more urgent in the face of the unprecedented, multilevelled survival crisis we now face. This desire for global relaxation causes me to travel all over the planet on a fairly consistent basis: writing, filming, recording music, giving talks, holding workshops, arranging musical events, working on creative collaborations, meeting with business people and working on all other means of getting the love – and its supercharged energy – out there.

I'm blessed to have the practical tools to help make all this a reality for people. The Taoist system I practise is possibly the most comprehensive and practical method of relaxation, energy production and mental-sharpening skills in the world today. I've spent most of my life living, breathing, eating and sleeping it; practising every day and teaching others how to do so too. And it works.

But I wouldn't want to force the Tao down anyone's throat. I appreciate that it's not for everyone, this way of the Taoist 'warrior'. It appeals to the maverick, the rebel, the individualist, the person who isn't willing to succumb to all the pretensions, lies and obfuscation of the everyday world. It's for those who seek the truth in all situations and want to feel authentic, relaxed, loving and beautiful in the midst of it all – connected to the spiritual source, yet fully engaged in the world, with its muck and mess, as much as with its miracles.

I grew up with a natural mystical tendency. I learned aikido at 11, became a hippie at 13, was drawn to Eastern-flavored philosophy, and got into yoga and tai chi in my late teens. In my early 20s I studied what I can only inadequately describe as life wisdom and consciousness with British psychiatrist R. D. Laing. When I lived in New Mexico in my mid- to late 20s, I studied acupuncture, Chinese medicine, Taoism and shamanism; and taught tai chi. In 1983, I started a healing practice in London, taught workshops and participated in experimental music events. I was, as far as I know, the first person in the UK (at a gig in London in 1985) and possibly the USA (at a gig in Greenwich Village the same year) ever to get large groups, sometimes with thousands of people, drumming together. It started off that whole tribal-drumming-for-enlightenment thing they use in corporate bonding sessions now. I taught tai chi and baby massage and kept the healing practice going up until 2000. After that, I got full-time into promoting the message through the media, making music, writing books, creating body products and coming up with all sorts of other offerings to spread the love.

In 1989, I started calling myself The Barefoot Doctor and inadvertently became a brand and someone with a profile as well, doing my level best to remain a regular person – or perhaps I should say an irregular one. Because although I have met real characters in my time and have hung out with mavericks of the highest order, eccentrics of the nuttiest variety, artists of the greatest originality and masters (and mistresses) of the most supreme wisdom and enlightenment, I've rarely met anyone with a life as varied, bizarre, unlikely – and as far as I'm concerned – as fulfilling and fun as my own.

And none of it would have happened or be happening now had I not been blessed to encounter such an unusual array of teachers.

Rather than being a self-centred biography, this book is an account of my interaction with those startling teachers and how they taught me to be the master of my own life. It's my sincere hope that my accounts of them serve to inspire you equally on your own path.

*** ***

Chapter One

Dance of the Red Ants

Dorset (near the coast of southern England), the summer of 1958: I'm four years old and standing on the red soil playing with pine cones while watching a tribe of red ants circling me. I've been bitten once on my heel and have cried loudly with the pain and shock, so I know the score with these little bastards. I feel a healthy respect for them and a healthy respect for myself, so I'm keen to assert my power and right to be there among them as an equal. I haven't yet been introduced to the dubious notion that humans are above all other living things. I simply don't want my freedom to move about the planet limited by a fear of red ants. I know that.

I find myself spontaneously tapping a rhythm with the cones on a large log as a way of communicating with them. It's a relatively complex, quasi-military beat, with a bit of a swing, intended to inspire respect. I'm aware I'm keeping perfect time, and that keeping perfect time is a skill and is important somehow. I know I've come into this lifetime with something I won't have to learn again, and I'm aware I'm doing magic.

When recounting my early memories, I've noticed that people are often surprised that I can remember so far back and in such detail. I'm equally surprised that they can't. These early memories comprise the most startling ones of our lives, and assuming we were awake and aware at the time, it should be perfectly natural to recall them with ease. They're the ones that have the initial impact on the way we form our views of the world and our place in it.

I say I'm surprised, but I'm not really. That's because I knew even back then that the majority of us go about in a trance most of the time and aren't actually aware of what's really going on at all. We're so concerned with playing the superficial, approval-seeking, punishment/reward game of local life effectively that even as babies we overlook the fact that the game is merely imaginary. It's just a way to pass the time while our spirits inhabit these bodies, until at some point in time and space, for whatever reason, they mysteriously relinquish them and move on.

I knew I was awake. I was aware of it from the first
thought I ever had, which was relatively unformulated,
but translated into 'adult' it went something like: *Damn,
this is cold and glaringly bright; how uncouth; what an
outrage.* This was as they held me upside down, fresh out
of my mother's womb, and slapped me callously to make
me cry, as they were accustomed to doing with amazing
insensitivity back then.

However, back to the beat – something it seems
we must each return to with regularity in some form
or another, if we wish to cooperate with the natural
regulatory forces of existence. I instinctively knew at the
age of four that rhythm was the palpable expression, at
the deepest level, of the universe in motion.

I can't say for sure whether this was entirely due to the
fact that my father was a jazz drummer and percussionist
and would spend much time drumming at home with
me sitting mesmerised, or whether it was actually an
inheritance from a former life. Indeed, perhaps it was a
neat combination of the two.

I do know that, at some point in every drumming
session, my father would teach me something: how to tap
'mummy-daddy', how to play a roll, how to accent the
roll and eventually how to get my hands around the left-
right-left-left, right-left-right-right pattern of the notorious
paradiddle at speed. But you can't effectively teach a
child, or anyone else, to do all that unless he or she
already has an instinct for the beat. He and I both knew it,

too, but neither of us ever commented on it. It was taken for granted in a father/son way, like taking a pee together and knowing you share the same genetic composition, and that your pee makes an arc in the air before splashing down . . .

Understand the rhythm of life – not intellectually, but by feeling it in your body – and you understand the rhythm of the way the forces of expansion and contraction, the yin and yang of Taoist philosophy, the zeros and ones of our present technological reality, alternate with each other. Understand that and you understand the rise and fall of fortune. Understand that and you have a chance of seeing through the everyday game to the eternal state behind it. Seeing through to eternity behind the game from moment to moment, you're liberated from the suffering that comes with being entranced. Furthermore, you're able to shift the actual conditions of the everyday, simply by perceiving them differently.

Right from the start I was eager to be liberated from suffering and to shift external conditions by magic (as I have no doubt we all are at some level). And I was eager to be doing it rather urgently with the red ants.

As I stood there among the red ants on the red soil with the red bite on my foot, instinctively banging out that beat with the pine cones on the log, causing reverberations in the ground to radiate in ever-increasing concentric circles (I could feel it), I noticed that the ants would keep a respectful distance. But when I stopped, they'd start moving dangerously toward me. It seemed obvious to me at that moment that such rhythmically induced vibration activation was a powerful tool for keeping the sting of life at bay, for keeping the disparate elements composing the everyday in order.

Not that I intellectualised it as such. I just knew it and accepted it. I also knew, from having experimented with sharing my findings, feelings, and rhythmic skills with my peers, that knowing and accepting your mysterious powers is not common. However, rather than dwelling on feeling different, I was always consumed with the desire to help those around me wake up to their own unique powers. Then I could have some fun with them in a way that was deeper than the relatively frivolous and superficial behaviourally conditioned variety generally on offer.

That urge to share the blessings so everyone could have more and more fun was always there, quite possibly also inherited from former lives; I don't know. Personally, I believe in past lives and hence, future ones, simply because it's easier to make sense of what appear to be the awful inequities of the world if you see this life as just one phase of many in the soul's eternal journey.

I realise that you're already wondering probably why I'm banging on about rhythm, excuse the pun, and what does that have to do with becoming a barefoot doctor, or more precisely for our purposes here, *The* Barefoot Doctor.

So let me first explain what a generic barefoot doctor is, or at least my interpretation of it.

BAREFOOT DOCTORS

Barefoot doctors were modest, noble, selfless characters who travelled humbly about the far-flung regions of ancient China and throughout Asia, their sole mission being to spread healing and cheerfulness wherever they went. I assume they were naturally enlightened beings, who, like me, didn't know how else to make a living. They weren't paid for their work directly. They were such folk heroes (or rather heroines, since most were actually women, whose roundedness of being was a prerequisite for such work) that they were supported by appreciative people wherever they went. The term *barefoot doctor* is simply a metaphor for these humble, wandering healers and doesn't imply that they were literally shoeless.

As necessary, they would perform acupressure or acupuncture; do massage and manipulations; dispense medicinal herbs; draw magical talismans on the walls of homes to attract good fortune and fertility; sing songs, play music, and use voice and rhythm in a quasi-shamanistic way with the help of lutes, flutes and percussion instruments; recite poetry to raise people's spirits; tell stories to illustrate Taoist philosophy and wisdom; and teach tai chi and chi-gung moves to make their devotees strong, clear and healthy.

When Chairman Mao and his crew got the run of China in 1949, they tended at first to throw out the baby with the bathwater in quite a big and splashy way, rejecting much of the magic and mystery of traditional Chinese medicine. It wasn't until somewhere around the mid-1970s that the then-mellowing great leader chose to reinvent and formalise the barefoot-doctor model as one made up of modern-day, white-coated medics. They were uniformed and uniformly trained and regulated to a viable standard, and obviously didn't employ or convey the same degree of Taoist-shamanistic magic or operate with the same depth of feeling as their namesakes. On the contrary, these were mostly men and veered strongly toward the technician style of practising medicine.

I never trained to become a barefoot doctor of either variety. I should also point out that when the term is used today, it doesn't imply that someone is trying to pass him- or herself off as a medical doctor. I have never wanted to be, or be thought of as, a medical doctor. If anything, I'm a magician rather than a technician. I have utmost respect for physicians because of their rigorous training and the irreplaceable function they fulfill, and count many of their number as my good friends and colleagues. I stand in relation to them as a little brother, here to offer what I can in a humble way to augment or supplement their fine work, if required.

Without design, I fell into learning the skills and tools that together consist of more-than-adequate qualifications for me to be called a barefoot doctor in the traditional sense. That includes drumming; playing the guitar, bass, harmonica, and keys; singing and chanting; composing music and poetry; writing essays and books; studying aikido, meditation, energy healing, yoga, psychotherapy, hypnotherapy, and relaxation; learning tai chi, Hsing I, and pa kua (the three Taoist internal martial arts); researching chi gung, red dragon (Taoist floor exercises), shamanism, acupuncture, acupressure, and herbs; practising Taoist massage and manipulation, polarity therapy, and Taoist magic (*wu-wei*); and divination using, among other things, the I-Ching and tarot; along with running, jumping and standing still.

I'd never intended to support myself from any of it – years ago, that sort of career path didn't exist in the conventional sense. It simply wouldn't have been seen as a feasible way to earn a living. The vocation aspect developed organically through my overriding enthusiasm for the traditions and techniques themselves, and an innate, almost childlike desire to share their fruits with one and all. I fell into teaching tai chi, for instance, because people saw me doing it and wanted me to teach *them*. I got into helping people in whatever way I could simply because the word spread that I had a way with the acupuncture needles. It all evolved naturally, rather than by contrivance.

Like the Fool in the tarot deck, I was just innocently following my fascination from day one with an insatiable lust for the keys to what I'd now call hyperreality, or the Tao, and it happened to lead me to learn these various arts and skills. It was in 1989 that I started calling myself The Barefoot Doctor. I was in a constant search for a simple, catch all job title to put on my business cards that would cover this plethora of skills I'd been blessed to have accrued. Also, the name would, coincidentally, double as a viable name for the band I had then.

Now I'm about to tell you the story of how I stumbled and bumbled along, following my fascination for life in all its aspects, and in doing so was led to meet and train with the most unlikely assortment of teachers, all of whom I consider to have been world class. This book is more the story of them and the wonderful gifts they passed on to me to make me the modern-day supercharged neo-Taoist Barefoot Doctor I am, than the definitive and racier personal autobiography I intend to write later.

The reason I'm doing so is to share some of the best of what I was so privileged to learn. This is for your benefit rather than for me to indulge in my personal story, although there's a fair bit of me in it. It would be hard to avoid that, as my presence was pivotal. I'm keen to do this because when I was journeying through it, the world was a far freer, more open-minded, more generous, less envy-ridden, less monetised, less litigious (and hence, less regulated and constricted) place than it currently is. This enabled teachers to be themselves and simply give of themselves and all their knowledge and power without the fear of being sued or hindered by unscrupulous individuals trying to con a moment of fame or a quick buck out of life. For this reason, modern-day training practices for people who wish to learn the magic of the ancient ways are necessarily bland by comparison, and I intend this book to be partly, by way of anecdotal antidote, a celebration of the old ways before they vanish forever in a sea of glossy style-over-substance banality.

And of all the wonderful, uninhibited teachers I was blessed to learn from, the most wonderful of all has to have been my own father.

I consider all the invaluable training I received from the rest, no matter their hugely esteemed status in my world or the world at large, to have been complementary to the inestimable, far-reaching life-training my father, Victor, gave me.

VICTOR THE VICTOR

Victor was a huge man. Not just in physical height, breadth, and depth, but in his capacity to love, in his levels of passion for life, in his natural common sense and wisdom, in his humour, in his generosity of spirit, in his warmth, and in his authenticity. He had a lot of soul.

On Sundays, at a certain point, Victor and I were in the habit of getting into the car and driving far away from our home in the hills of North London to the countryside. He'd have music playing on the radio. Bebop and hard bop were his thing, but he enjoyed all genres and would use these opportunities to teach me about whatever was playing. He'd explain how a band was structured and how a piece of music is like a mathematical journey through the realms of the soul. Interspersed with and set against the backdrop of chat about a particular song or style, these car-borne interludes also provided an opportunity for my early training in accommodating the existential paradox.

'If I'm me and you're you,' he'd ask with faux seriousness, 'who are you?'

'I'm me,' I'd respond, generally in squeals of laughter because I knew what was coming.

'No, I'm me. Who are you?'

'I'm you,' I'd reply.

'No, I'm me. Who are you?'

'I'm me and you and neither' was about the cleverest I ever got about it, and that wasn't until I was an adult. And there was always that wonderful gap created by the Zen-like koan – that vacuum of no identity and non-understanding, but of glimpsing the paradox. Because of my father's warmth, remaining in this existentially unresolved state with him felt exciting, safe, and proper. Being both stirred by and comfortable with the paradox – not seeking resolution but allowing resolution to come of itself if at all – constitutes major wisdom. Victor gave me this.

Then there was the boxing. Victor was a consummate boxer. He'd been a champion in the Army and regularly taught me the moves: feinting, blocking, jabbing with the left, docking with the right, nimble footwork and so on. The way he taught, although on the brusque side, made it such fun that I formed an addiction to boxing, or more precisely, to the adrenaline rush it caused. So much so that by the time I was 10, I was getting into trouble at school for being a bit of a terror, which led me to take up aikido at his suggestion when I was 11.

There was a paradox in this boxing training, too. Victor had been disturbed by World War II in general as a child of the London blitz, and specifically by seeing his older brother return from the front in Europe. He'd been in intelligence there, had witnessed and no doubt taken part in unspeakable horrors and had returned to civilian life cold, hard-hearted, and altogether alienated. So Victor had an innate abhorrence for human violence and cruelty. He always ended every boxing session with admonishments not to be violent or cruel, but always to be loving, even in a fight . . . in other words, just what they tell you in tai chi training.

One day when I was about seven, this paradox came alive before my startled eyes. The two of us were walking into the office of a friend of Victor's while engrossed in conversation about whether either of us was jealous of the Beatles, who had just exploded onto the scene and were living the dream. We were discussing how envy was a waste of time because we each have our own destiny and must make the best of it, being grateful for every little thing. Absorbed in the discussion, Victor happened to step in some wet concrete being laid by two burly workmen at the entrance.

'Stupid c---', one of them muttered loud enough for us both to hear.

Suddenly the world stopped still. A silence ensued, probably lasting a second but which seemed to go on for about 30 minutes.

'What did you say?!' Victor asked in a voice a bit like a volcano about to erupt.

'Fu—' started the cockier of the two, but before he'd had time to get to the '—ck off', Victor landed a spontaneous right hook so powerful it knocked the guy to the ground. The other one backed off, clearly afraid. And then a remarkable thing happened. Victor leaned down and, with the most amazing care and compassion I'd ever seen, helped up the guy he'd just hit. He apologised for punching him, explaining how he didn't want his kid to be exposed to that kind of language. The guy, recognising humaneness, apologised, and they shook hands warmly, like brothers.

Then in front of them both, he said to me, 'I'm ashamed of that, Steve. I acted like an animal. There's nothing clever in it.'

When we came out of the building a bit later, all four of us shook hands as if we were old friends.

Naturally, the incident had a powerful impact on me. Being exposed to fully grown men dropping the thin veneer of socialisation and expressing their primal side was a shock, but even then I knew it was a healthy one. Of course, Victor helped me in this understanding by being able to include me as an adult and by admitting to his faults rather than doing what most would do: continue asserting their reasons for being right rather than wrong.

Admitting to one's own faults was a big thing with him.

Admitting to what he was feeling was a big thing with him.

Being himself with people and not acting or pretending was a big thing with him.

Leaving people feeling better about themselves than before they encountered him was a big thing with him.

Cracking gags at every opportunity and so transforming hardships into humour was a big thing with him.

Being present and doing whatever he was doing with passion and soul was a big thing with him.

Being extraordinarily pragmatic was a big thing for him.

And all these big things naturally became big things for me too, at an early age. I was privileged in that sense, and I knew it.

This isn't to say that my mother didn't have her big things, too: integrity, honesty, and dignity, to name just three. But somehow, my relationship with my mother was so close-up and, as a small child, so mystical and all-embracing, that it was hard to see her as a teacher. My father, on the other hand, being more of an exotic figure, perhaps on account of only being home some of the time, filled the role more easily for me.

Along with all the more unusual gifts I inherited from Victor, came the usual fatherly offerings, such as teaching me to ride a bike. From that grew my love of freedom and travel, for as soon as I was balancing on my bicycle, I was off exploring the streets like there was no tomorrow. As amazing as it sounds now, in those days it was more or less safe for small children to be out on their own in the streets of North London. These days they wouldn't last more than five minutes without either being kidnapped or enlisted as drug runners, or both.

Teaching me to swim and dive was another gift from Victor. He'd been a local breaststroke champion at one time. He spent hours teaching it to me as well as the crawl, backstroke, and butterfly. The day I 'got' it and could finally divest myself of water wings was one of the most beautifully rewarding moments of my life. Second to that was the day I could finally dive; third was the day I could swim underwater the length of an Olympic-sized pool; and fourth was the day he taught me to waterski. The rewards were the connectedness with my dad as much as achieving the goals in each project.

Yes, it's true I loved that guy. He was, and remains, my most esteemed hero.

However, probably the most adroit move he ever made in terms of my life path was to encourage me to take up aikido when I was 11. But before I relate that story, let me go back and tell you about the time I heard the sacred *Om* when I was six, because it was probably the greatest life-shaping event I experienced up until now.

*** ***

Chapter Two

The Sacred *Om*

It's late afternoon, and I'm just back from school. I'm lying on my bed watching the clouds go by in the North London sky outside the window. I'm in an everyday state of mind, nothing particularly altered about it. All I've eaten is some jam sandwiches, and there wasn't anything 'funny' about them.

All of a sudden, with no warning or fanfare, I hear an all-consuming sub-bass register rumble as big, wide, and loud as the universe itself. It sounds like a million lamas chanting *om*, transposed approximately 50 octaves below normal human hearing levels. Although epic in scale and amplitude, it's also subtle enough to fit between my ears and not be heard by anyone else at that moment. I know this without a doubt.

I also know that I'm not suffering the effects of a sonic hallucination or inner-ear trouble, nor am I imagining it.

Immediately, without questioning, in that innocent, knowing way that children possess, I understand that this is God speaking. (I didn't have exotic names for the divine, like the Tao, at hand in those days.) At least it's the *sound* of God talking because it isn't made up of words as far as I can hear, yet somehow it contains all the information in existence. I know that, too.

I'm aware that I'm the only one hearing this. I'm also certain that there's no point rushing to tell my mother who's downstairs, not because she'll think I'm mad, but because it simply won't mean anything to her. It won't fit in her frame of reference.

I have no idea why this is happening, but it isn't a surprise. I notice that I'm not even shocked by it. It feels like a natural extension of being able to hold a beat. I realise that I'm privileged to hear it and instinctively think I'm hearing it to remind me that I have this connection, and this connection is the most precious gift I have. Also, I know that the way I'm going to contribute to this world is going to somehow involve sharing the keys to this connection so that everyone can enjoy it as much as I do, because by now I'm already well aware of how enjoyable it is. Every time it comes over me – and it's like a wave coming out of the blue, although up till now never with sound – my face tingles, and I feel an immense excitement in my chest unlike any other.

After what feels like an eternity, but which in linear time is probably no more than a few seconds, the sound recedes and I return to 'normal' in that wonderfully innocent way kids do.

In my subsequent studies as an adult, I learned that in India there is a yoga practice of sound, the point of which is to discern the subtle *shabd,* the sacred sound that underpins existence. It turns out that this phenomenon has been mapped by physicists who reckon the entire universe is built on a sound wave 50 octaves below human hearing levels.

I still don't know why I heard it, but I've discovered over the years that 'Why?' is mostly a pointless question anyway. 'How?' generally throws up more interesting answers, and I've been dedicated to studying and providing as many ways to make the connection as I can for the last 30 years or more. I do know that hearing the sacred *om* was connected to my love of making music, which was starting to happen around that time with the magical introduction of the guitar to my list of things to make noise with.

SIX STRINGS

'There are six strings,' said James Royce, unquestionably one of the most compassionate and understanding music teachers of all time, stating the obvious and starting with the basics. 'Feel them – go on, touch them one by one.'

He got me, with my slightly nervous seven-year-old fingers, to caress that guitar before I even played a note.

'It's all about tone,' he offered. 'Get the right tone and it doesn't matter what note you play – it will sound good. And to get the right tone, you have to love the guitar. Love it and touch it as if it were a person.' Then he looked at me, miming the shape of the guitar and smiling. 'As if it were a woman.' I blushed. I got what he meant.

He didn't think I had the temperament to be a classical player but told me that if I wanted, he'd teach me all the chords I'd need to play blues and rock and roll. I very much did! He said he'd teach me how to pick and strum, and if after that I wanted to take things further and commit to learning scales, we could discuss it. James was in his early 20s, and I could tell he was definitely an evolved and groovy guy disguised as a school music teacher. I felt great warmth and respect for him. This was because of the unusual warmth and respect he showed me, rather than trying to frighten me into submission, as most other schoolteachers I'd encountered until then had tried in vain to do. I wanted to work hard to fulfil my end of the deal because I believed that if someone was taking the time to teach me from the heart, I owed it to him (or her) to do my bit and practise what he was teaching me assiduously enough to make it my own.

Another great gift James bestowed upon me was the willingness and capacity to both improvise and make up chord progressions, and eventually create tunes of my own, rather than fixating on copying others. He explained how every musician was influenced by other musicians, but to copy others cut one off from the divine source from which the music originated.

In the process of demonstrating how music was a channel to the divine, he'd play me extracts of various recordings – mostly classical – explaining that even though I wasn't interested in it, classical music was the mother of everything subsequent. At least this was the case in the Western idiom. If I had a feel for that, he said, I'd have a proper grounding. And so I was exposed to many of the 'best bits' of Bach, Haydn, Beethoven, Sibelius, Strauss (Richard), Stravinsky, and so on. Meanwhile, on the other side of things, Victor was turning me on to the likes of Billy Preston, Jimmy Smith, Aretha Franklin, Little Richard, Dusty Springfield, and most importantly, the Beatles.

I always thought it would have been so much easier had music been the whole story for me, as I would have focused on just that and would have had a far simpler time of things. But I was too fascinated by the underlying mechanics of existence and consciousness – of which music and sound were clearly just one expression – to be satisfied channelling all my attention into that.

I knew all of that instinctively, too.

PUCCINI TO PUGILISM

While I was attuned to this deeper level of reality and fully aware of how privileged I was to do so, I was otherwise what you'd think of as a normal little boy and did all the things that kids do. I had friends, I had fun, I made mischief, I laughed and giggled, I ran and played, I rode my bike . . . and I also fought.

From what seemed like out of nowhere and everywhere at once, I found myself a compulsive pugilist. Of course it was connected with my dad teaching me to box, but my fighting seemed to come from somewhere else altogether. It wasn't at all due to any particular desire to be cruel or inflict pain, but simply from a desire to feel that adrenaline flowing. It was definitely triggered the first time the school bully started in on me, as I just let it rip and then watched him run. I admit now that I also enjoyed the respect this simple reaction earned me from my peers, but I wasn't aware of that at the time. I was just going on automatic. The more fights I could initiate thereafter, the happier I seemed to feel; fortunately, no one ever got seriously hurt. Then one day – I'd just turned 11 – the headmaster called my parents; and I was subject to that first big, existentially head-twisting, stomach-churning, reality-checking reprimand that I assume every child experiences at some point at the hands of concerned adults.

Victor set about trying to figure out a way to calm me down and somehow channel my pugilistic tendencies.

Then purely by chance, although some might say divine design, a good friend of his came by the house raving about some Japanese martial arts master who taught a relatively new practice called *aikido,* and it was soon decided that this would be the perfect thing for me.

EXPECTING THE UNEXPECTED

So there I am, standing eagerly and a bit sheepishly in my crisp virgin-white *gi* and my pure-white beginner's belt tied around my waist as instructed. This little, old-, strange-, scary-, but somehow kind-looking Japanese man called Tio or Tayo (take your pick, but say it gutturally from between your legs for the authentic sound) is inspecting my chest intensely as if he can see right through my skin. Then he looks deep into my eyes to the back of my skull. No one has ever done this to me before, except the occasional doctor examining me when I've had mumps or whatever, and I'm not sure whether to smile politely or remain expressionless. I flit nervously between the two for a while until he grunts affirmatively, saying, 'Good, very good. No diseases.'

I'm happy to hear it. I instinctively know that he knows what he's talking about and don't even think to question why he's examined me in the first place (I'm assuming it has to do with quality control). He's been described ahead of time as a healer and martial arts master. Both of these sound exotic enough to grab my attention, although the healer aspect feels a bit creepy. I overlook that and cast it to one side of my mind until I subsequently discover that it's all about this mysterious *ki,* rather than a mysterious faith of any kind. I've been transported to an alternative reality, and I'm expecting the unexpected. It feels okay, and I accept it freely without feeling the need to question any of it – or him – too much. (This is a strategy that has occasionally let me down in life since then. Nonetheless, I'm glad to state that I've largely stuck to it, as it's been a largely successful approach.)

Tio then goes on to explain *ki* (*chi,* or life force) and its use in self-defence, as well as in healing people and even making magic happen. I'm transfixed and sold on the spot – I want some; I want all of it, if possible. I'm fully aware at the time that wanting it as much as I do is remarkable in some way and extremely important to me, although I don't bother trying to understand why.

Why would I? I'm only 11 and, as I said, careers like mine hadn't been invented yet, other than in the traditional sense. I was a first.

Tio makes a theatrical gesture and pumps his whole body up a few sizes, transforming from a fairly ordinary size to XXXL superhuman in an instant. It's a good trick and one I think I might try in front of the bathroom mirror when I get home later. (I did, but found it didn't work for me and was both disappointed yet pleased that it hadn't been just a cheap trick.)

Tio grunts and points. 'Punch me hard in the belly –
here.' He knows my story and understands that I consider
myself a boxer. With his smile, he's inviting me to show
him my worst.

'Really?' My tremulous, perplexed, yet increasingly
curious voice pipes up.

'Punch!' He says it in such a commanding way I don't
think to refuse.

I try to give it my all but falter. It feels too strange, and I
pull my punch at the last moment, only landing about 30
per cent of my force.

'Punch!' He grunts even louder.

So I let go and lob one in, harder than any punch in
my personal history.

And nothing.

It's like punching a large balloon. Nothing happens.

My hand doesn't hurt; his belly evidently doesn't hurt.
Only my brain hurts a bit from being unable to compute
what has just happened.

'Ki!' he grunts, and laughs resoundingly.

And so it begins.

I am mesmerised, awestruck. I'll do anything this man
tells me to, and I'll learn everything he wants to teach me
for ever and ever. I will not resist.

I notice my mind making these choices quite clearly,
and wise ones they turned out to be.

This is the first time in my young life that I don't
feel the instinctual urge to ridicule, rebel, resist, or in

any other way throw a wrench in the works when an authoritarian adult, other than my dad, has tried to coerce me into submission regardless of the goodness of the intention. But this isn't coercion. This is like dealing with someone who has a nuclear arsenal hidden up their *gi*. There's simply no point even questioning it: you either run away and never come back, or you do it his way.

I don't run.

Tio's way, it turns out, involves an implausible number of repetitions of squats, frog jumps, push-ups, sit-ups, side stretches, hip stretches, hamstring stretches, and paradigm stretches. It also includes long, fast, nauseating runs around the park in very cold weather while throwing, grappling, falling, and rolling quickly from position to position – occasionally taking an errant punch or kick that overcomes any amount of resolve not to stand there blubbering like a baby. Then there was the sitting for fairly long periods, listening to the sound of an old clock ticking almost excruciatingly loudly in an otherwise silent room, where I was instructed to think about absolutely nothing except the 'one point,' the *hara* or *tanden* (*tan t'ien,* or lower energy centre just below the navel) . . . when I wasn't thinking about who I'd like to use this shit on once I got back out on the street. Then, at the end of every session, as if by way of antidote to the aggressive urge and to quell such monkey-minded thoughts, Tio demonstrated how to channel *ki* down the arms and through the palms or

fingers with a view to using it compassionately in order
to bring healing to people in pain.

As I was the only kid Tio was teaching, he started me
off with a series of one-on-one sessions until he felt I was
ready to take a grading (or ranking) and join his class of
what was then only adult males. (Outside of judo, not
many women participated in martial arts in the UK in
those days, and in fact, not many men did either – and
certainly very few boys.)

I soon became the class mascot, and everything was
going well until the day we were to practise a technique
to defend ourselves against three attackers at once. It's a
great move. You wait for them to be nearly upon you, then
using their incoming force, you slither down like a snake
and explode suddenly into a double-fisted uppercut under
the chin of the guy immediately in front of you, followed
swiftly by bilateral punches, effectively breaking the
middle attacker's windpipe and destroying the testicles
and any further reproductive potency of the two at the
sides. This, of course, works provided that your attackers
position themselves in the right spots (one of the pitfalls in
basic-level martial arts training as opposed to boxing, in
my opinion).

The trouble occurred when it was my turn to play
one of the sidekicks. I was slightly smaller than the other
'attackers' because I was no more than a third of their
age. Consequently, the defender's side punches – which
were meant to be aimed in the air between the legs of the

pretend assailants so as not to cause damage – managed to catch me square in the balls with such concentrated force that I couldn't speak, I couldn't even cry, I simply couldn't do anything . . . for quite a while. Then Tio walked over to my stunned self and put his hand in front of my crotch from a short distance away. He blasted me with energy, which almost instantly eliminated the pain, and I was miraculously back in the fray as if nothing had happened.

As well as making me a little more conscious of how I positioned and protected my manhood – or more accurately, boyhood – in relation to potential attackers, this also introduced me to the incontrovertible miracle of the healing power of *ki, chi, qi,* or whatever you want to call it.

More than the tumbling, more than the rolling, more than the grappling and even more than the throwing, this seemed to have the greatest impact on my psyche. The meditation did too, and I already saw how healing people was just meditating, and directing the power their way instead of within. I set about offering healing to anyone who was game enough to try it.

It was fun to watch how people reacted – sceptical and indulgent of a child at first – but then astonished when their headache cleared up or their back stopped hurting. It became even more fun as my teenage years progressed, affording me access to the inner sanctum of all the best spoiled-prettiest-girl-at-the-party-throwing-a-fit

melodramas that had a habit of developing at gatherings
of my peers with all those hormones flying about. I also
gained privileged insight into how, beneath the bluster,
bravado and adult façade, everyone is really just a baby
crying in fear and bewilderment at finding him- or herself
at large in the big, bad world.

So I have much to thank Tio for. He introduced me to
the concepts of psycho-physical discipline, self-discipline,
self-defence, quiet confidence, *ki,* stilling the mind and
being organised around a physical centre. And he also
opened the way for me to one day become a healer,
specifically as a day job for 17 years, and subsequently in
the broadest sense.

As for the reason that got me to him in the first place
– my hotheaded nature – his training started working
efficaciously almost from day one. Although I'd leave every
lesson just praying for someone to start on me so I could
try out the moves in real life, no one ever did. The rule that
Tio's teachings must only be used in self-defense, never
to initiate fights, was so inculcated in my circuits from the
start by this stupendously powerful teacher that I never
thought about transgressing. In fact, I never started a fight
again and am proud to say that the only times I've had to
use martial arts over the years have been to stop a couple
of street fights: to defend against a drunk who came at me
and to scare off someone who threatened me with a knife.

I hope never to be called upon to use any of it at
all in the future, other than in the most benign and

discreet ways. That's because all the masters say that if you actually find yourself using this stuff, you've made your first big mistake. The idea is to develop such inner poise, and hence, power, that the atmosphere becomes absolutely peaceful and the people fully amenable wherever you go, without your doing a thing to make it so.

So I'm eternally indebted to Tio for introducing, or rather from the eternal viewpoint, reintroducing, me to the Asian martial arts. Without a doubt, they form at least a sizable proportion of my make-up in the deepest sense.

Oddly enough, in its quirky way, music played a part even in this rare dynamic.

In fact, beyond all the profound thrills of experiencing the finely and naturally engineered altered states associated with learning martial arts, meditation, and healing for the first time, the most memorable encounter I had with Tio was when, for some inexplicable reason, he invited me into his inner sanctum. It was a small, stuffy den with a large antiquated record player and a hefty collection of old LPs. He had me sit in an overstuffed armchair and listen attentively to a scratchy 78 recording of some long-forgotten Russian male classical singer.

Bear in mind that I was 12 at the time and strongly into the Beatles, the Rolling Stones, Jimi Hendrix, Cream, Pink Floyd, and so on. Also, Stan Getz was my dad's cousin, so *bossa nova* was held sacred as part of the listening curriculum at home, as was bebop and hard bop (because of my dad's addiction to it), along with the odd bit of Beethoven, Bach and that crew.

So having to listen to what at the time I would have called 'a load of scratchy, old shit of the weirdest sort' wasn't easy on me, but in no way would I have thought of declining this invitation into Tio's personal space—it was an honour even if the music was a tad turgid to my ears.

Then a remarkable thing happened. Within the field of Tio's power, I found myself entering into the spirit of the scratchy, weird shit I was listening to and *loving* it. That was a breakthrough for me. It opened the door to appreciating Stockhausen, Thelonius Monk, and all the other composers and players who are ingenious but who make music that's more or less impossible to tap your feet to, let alone get up and dance to. Still, their input has been essential to the evolution of modern music, especially in the world of electronica and quasi-electronica that I deal in myself.

It keeps coming back to sound.

*** ***

Chapter Three

Swinging London

From about the age of 11, possibly because of being exposed to the so-called adult world through aikido, certainly because I tended to find conversation with people my own age somewhat limited in range and scope, I tended to hang out a lot with people much older than I was. I was tall for my age and relatively physically mature, so I could pass for being older (a trend that my tai chi practice fortunately reversed for me in later years). I was able to slide into the scene going on in London from an early age – and what a scene it was at the height of the 'swinging '60s' and the 'underground movement' they spawned. All kinds of people were experimenting with all kinds of things to engender altered states in order to know and feel the divine truth behind the charade of everyday reality. Sadly, so much of this spirit has been subsequently muffled, and that's why it's central to my work to do what I can to keep that flame burning today.

MURRAY THE HIPPIE

I'm 12, going on 13, and I'm down near Felixstowe on the coast of England at a summer camp for teens. Already I'm taken by the mystical aspect of reality, while naturally drawn to the main game going on – that is, connecting intimately with people of the opposite sex. But just like all the other kids, my fascination is with the curious character that everyone's calling Murray the Hippie, who's a bit older and wiser looking than the rest of us: he's the grand age of 14. Everyone shuns him because he smokes dope and wears strange clothing – both relatively new habits to the culture at the time. He also has mysterious dark circles around his eyes, making him look a bit worse for wear but decidedly dangerously deep. In addition to smoking hash and looking odd, he listens to underground music that no one has heard of yet – Cream, Love, Spooky Tooth – and wanders around appearing very happy with himself as if he knows something that others don't.

Over the days, my fascination grows so strong that I simply have to approach him and ask if I can try some dope. To be honest, he doesn't encourage my enthusiasm and indeed does everything he can to dissuade me. Looking back, though, this might have been less about him not wishing to be a bad influence as much as not wanting to spark a craze and end up giving away his entire stash.

In any case, I finally convince Murray of my integrity in wanting to experience the THC-induced altered state that people have been going on about, telling him that I do aikido and meditate and am not just seeking a cheap thrill. We agree to meet the following afternoon at a shed in the Magic Garden, a magnificent Victorian rose garden.

I arrive duly nervous, as if going for a skills evaluation in aikido. The amazing thing is that when he opens the little matchbox he keeps the hash in and unwraps it from its silver foil, I know the smell of it as well as I know the smell of bacon and eggs. But there's absolutely no way I have ever smelled it before in this life. This is something I now firmly attribute to a past life in India, where mothers put hashish in their baby's milk to calm them.

Murray rolls a joint, explaining how I have to hold the smoke in so the THC can circulate to my brain properly. He gets me doing what I now know as *pranayama* – breathing exercises to expand the lung capacity – and we set about smoking the hash.

The next four hours are without doubt the most magical, enjoyable, colourful, sense-enhanced, amusing, riveting, and illuminating of my life so far. (I'm not sure if this still holds true but am fairly sure it does, which reveals that I haven't exactly had a dearth of magical experiences since.)

It's as if a veil has been lifted from my senses: I can see colours more vividly, hear sounds more clearly, and can even tune in to the music of the world playing through the blare of cars moving along the road. And I'm laughing almost uncontrollably; not just mindlessly, but because all at once I see the joke. Everyday life is just an illusion, and everyone is engaged in upholding the charade without even knowing it. This makes me laugh so hard my sides are splitting, and every time I look at Murray, I get worse, so he forbids me to look at him. Of course I rebel against that and my sides are hurting, but I can't stop. We go out to the nearby town and meander around, stumbling across the local cinema. They're showing the Beatles' movie *Yellow Submarine,* which has just come out. It couldn't be more perfect, so we go in and lose ourselves in the colours and sound.

After we come out, Murray shows me how, by seeming to run your fingers down the length of someone's arm half an inch away, the person can feel it as clearly as if you're actually touching him or her. This is also strangely familiar to me, but not because of the energy channelling I'm learning from Tio. I'm 12 going on 13 and not connecting things just yet. In any case, the energy channelling I'm learning doesn't involve stroking the auric aspect of meridians. I seem to recognize this from somewhere else and am excited about it. In fact, I'm buzzing so much –

feeling the *chi* moving down my arm under his fingers like a magnet moving a ball bearing – that I can hardly contain myself.

The afternoon's entertainment ends with a quantum leap in the scope of my musical universe when Murray introduces me to the new blues of Cream and what I recognise as the Stockhausen-influenced sound of *The Piper at the Gates of Dawn* by Pink Floyd. This is the instant the world of the mystical East and the so-called hippie underground fuses for me. I don't know it at the time, but it turns out to be a crucially defining moment in shaping what I'm going to offer and how I'm going to present it to the world.

The dynamics back at the camp were interesting to observe after that.

At first people looked at me a bit suspiciously: I'd gone over to the other side. But within a short while, as they noticed I hadn't gone insane, become a heroin addict or slid down any other slippery slope, they all started wanting to know about hash and asking me to introduce them to Murray the Hippie so they could try it too. Murray naturally made himself scarce – again, admirable for not wishing to gain kudos as most 14-year-olds would, or at least for having the sense not to open himself up to having to give away all his hash for the sake of fleeting popularity.

When my mother picked me up from Liverpool Street Station, she didn't even say hello. She just looked at me from 20 feet away and sternly demanded, 'What's happened to you?' It's amazing how mothers can tell.

What had happened to me was that I'd woken up to the illusion of everyday life, and I soon discovered that there was a whole world of people out there in London who not only knew the joke too, but had also turned celebrating it into an art form, which was made up of colour, sound, ancient mystical symbols of the East, and the smell of patchouli.

Although I was a kid, relatively speaking, I was still pretty clued-in, streetwise and lifewise, and able to hold my own around older folks. I made it my mission to explore this underground world and find the jewel hidden in its depths, wherever that might be: in smoky clubs, ear-pounding gigs, darkly lit flats in Notting Hill, or hanging around at Kensington Market or the Eros statue in Piccadilly Circus whiling away the time in collective contemplation and saying 'Yeah, man' a fair bit, as hippies did in those days.

I discovered that no one knew where the jewel was or even what it was. That mystery was going to take a while longer to reveal itself to the world. People knew it had something to do with love and peace, meditation, relaxation, seeing through the illusion, engendering altered states, and being helpful to each other; but few yet knew quite how to achieve all that. The methods were only just revealing themselves.

However, I was seeing that there could be a way to make it easy. Based on my experience to date, I made up a spiritual discipline I called 'God of the Mind'. I sculpted a little Buddha-like statue from clay and erected a small altar to it where I'd sit and meditate each day. It only attracted one other adherent – my friend Rob – and then only for an hour or so. He quickly grew bored, and we went out instead. I realised then that the meditative path wasn't for everyone.

People in those days often augmented their experimenting with LSD and cannabis, but essentially, a rediscovery of the ancient ways was going on. This was the forerunner of what we now think of as the self-development industry, except folks then weren't looking at it so much for outer profit as much as to discover their inner prophet.

One of the more ancient ways to achieve this wavelength was by using tone, metre and rhythm along with the voice to induce states of deep relaxation and wholeness in others. Incorporating the drum with this makes up the basis of shamanism. It's the precursor to modern hypnotherapy and its offshoots such as NLP (neuro-linguistic programming), EFT (emotional freedom techniques) and the other ubiquitous three-letter acronyms flying carefree around the marketplace these days.

I was no stranger to the concept of hypnotherapy or trance due to my meditation training and musical background, the drumming, my incursions into underground venues, as well as my own investigations into the world of psychology – having been an avid reader on the subject since I was 11. (That age was clearly a watershed year for me in the existential department.) But I was 14 when I was taken to Roger Firestone's place one evening by a mutual friend – and bear with me here, as we're about to undergo a random flip out of the usual linear time sequence, simply because I have him on my mind and wish to give his story some air.

ROGER FIRESTONE

I'm not sure of the origins of the old military use of the phrase *Roger that* when replying in the affirmative to a request, but I love to use it myself whenever I can. It makes me giggle inside. Possibly for this reason, or possibly not, the first time I actually met anyone named Roger, I was instantly open to him in the sense of finding myself spellbound and innately positive.

It was ironic how I met Roger Firestone, considering the profound effect he had on my life. I was hanging out with undoubtedly my most superficial friend at the time, a guy I'd go out with whenever I was in the mood for some trivial fun. One night, as we were driving around town in his convertible sports car, honking at all the pretty girls and generally making mischief, he suddenly turned to me and said, 'You like all that psychological stuff. Let's go and visit my golf buddy, Roger: he's into all that stuff, too.'

Roger was instantly calming to be around. We spoke quite a bit and soon got onto the topic of the wonders of hypnosis. (Bear in mind that there wasn't the plethora of glossy magazines and daytime TV shows going on about every 'new' variety of so-called alternative medicine like there is today. Back then, we weren't bombarded with people pushing ancient methods that had been repackaged and given catchy names.) This stuff was genuinely exciting and, as I said, people weren't into it for the career move. It was innocent fascination and intrepid exploration of uncharted frontiers of the human psyche, at least for us in the West. And there's nothing much more exciting than that.

I was at peak levels of existential excitation the moment I walked into Roger's place and asked him to put me under hypnosis without delay.

He explained that he would only put me in a light trance, since it was the first time. I'd be fully cognisant of what was going on, yet simultaneously in an altered state similar to having smoked cannabis but without the potential mood distortion. Roger used the traditional counting-down induction, taking me slowly from ten to one and into a light trance state, one totally familiar if subtly distinct in tone from the *ki* meditation I was learning with Tio. He got me to meet my innermost

limitless self, the *atman,* and have a good chat with it
in order to address my deepest fears and become more
fearless in my life. Then Roger deftly brought me back out
into the everyday state, feeling refreshed and rejuvenated.

'You've got to teach me that. That was fucking
amazing!' I declared in all my youthful exuberance.

And he agreed.

So once a week for a few weeks, I'd show up at his
place and have a session – first him on me and then me
on him – with a little chat to follow. And then I'd go and
practise on anyone who'd let me. Again, I must stress in
the context of this over-regulated world we currently live
in that none of this was with a view to making a career. I
had an utter fascination for how it all worked, combined
with an innate urge to share the joy with those around me.

Even more crucially, this wasn't about learning a
technique as much as it was about my soul attuning to
Roger's. That's what constitutes true learning, which,
after all, is merely being reminded of what you already
know. And Roger had a fine soul to attune with, as well
as a wonderful manner and beautifully relaxing speaking
voice. He was an utter inspiration to the point of being a
full-on hero and role model to me.

In his late 20s at the time, Roger was the archetypal
hippie who had it all (and then some): kindness; wisdom;
looks; brains; wealth; personality; soul; long, black curly
hair; and a bottle-green convertible Rolls-Royce Corniche.
You can't top a combo like that.

One of my more glorious moments playing with the essentially Ericksonian progressive-relaxation method he taught me was when I was nearly 15, a few months after meeting him. I was spending the summer in Munich at the home of a friend's family. Subsequent to the feat of breaking through the linguistic barrier (I'd been learning German at school but now had to learn it for real), I found myself doing the relaxation induction (in fluent German) while softly picking out entrancing arpeggios on an acoustic guitar to an impromptu gathering of about 20 other kids at a party one night.

I thought I was the bee's knees for that – and still do, as it happens.

ROGER HOLMES

Before I move too far away from this era, and while on the subject of Rogers, I must also mention Roger Holmes, my English teacher. While I was beginning to explore the fascinating world of the underground scene, paradoxically, I was also doing extremely well in school. By 12 years old, I'd finally done all the 'bucking up' that my headmasters, teachers, and parents had been urging; and one of the areas I seemed to be excelling in most was English, specifically writing poetry and prose. This was very much because of Roger H., who was without a doubt one of the scariest yet most brilliant teachers the world has ever spawned – and not least because he recognised a talent in me and encouraged it consistently. He was never one for a gratuitous smile or *bon mot,* but he had so much personal presence that he was able to freeze his students on the spot with just a glance. I didn't work hard to earn a smile from him; I did it to avoid the freeze-out look.

Roger H. spent a good amount of time earnestly teaching Tennyson. Then only after we'd sweated and struggled with it did he close the book and say, 'Rubbish. Ponderous rubbish, Tennyson. This is what to avoid. Lightly, lightly stroke the page with your words. Let each one sing in a sweet tone. Hear the sound of each here.' He tapped the centre of his forehead.

And I got it. I loved the irreverence, and the tension and release of it, which is what set me off writing. What's interesting, though, is how everything linked back to sound.

SIDNEY THE KIDNEY

Also around this time, my father, a keen people-watcher, fan of Desmond Morris (author of the 1967 bestseller *The Naked Ape*) and avid buff of human psychology, had a friend he called Sidney the Kidney. He was a psychiatrist who lived in Highgate in North London, and the two of them would often while away the hours discussing the ins and outs of egos and ids, the conscious, and the subconscious. I'm not really sure whether Victor took me to Sidney's for dinner one night because he wanted to expand my awareness of the mechanics of reality and mind, or if it was to have me informally checked out, just to be sure all this hippie stuff I was into was safe. Neither of them is around now to ask.

Sidney was a master of loosening the tongue. I found myself spontaneously launching into a lengthy monologue about myself, the scene, the mind, people, my beliefs, meditation, aikido, healing, hypnosis, sexual politics, drugs, the illusion of everyday life and all the rest in far more depth and detail than I'd have offered my dad under normal circumstances. Making these disclosures was a risk. When I was done, I was suddenly aware of myself again. There was a silence that seemed to go on for a couple of days, although in reality, it was a couple of seconds at most. Sidney the Kidney started laughing louder and louder, then Victor started, and then I did. The three of us were rolling about for a while, wiping tears from our eyes.

'He's perfectly sane,' Sydney assured my dad in a brief interval, and then the hysterics started all over again.

Now I have no idea whether S the K knew he was providing me with a major life-forming moment. But to reveal your entire cosmological model to an expert of the mind (and such a wise and kindly one as he) at such a young age and be assured that it was sound, albeit going fully against the conventional grain at the time, was a gift of epic proportions. It's been something that has stood me in good stead ever after, which is important when one works on the forefront of human consciousness as I do, where tests to the validity of your model and your underlying levels of sanity are rife at every turn.

SID, THE BARBER OF COMMERCIAL ROAD

And while we're on the Sidneys of this world, it's fitting for me to tell you about Sid, the barber of Commercial Road. My grandfather was a proper cockney, defined as having grown up in the East End of London within shouting distance of Bow Bells. He was handsome and dapper; and used to have a shave, trim, and manicure once a week at Sid the Barber's. He continued to do this throughout his life. In fact, he even kept going back to Sid's long after he moved away to the 'Holy Hills' of North London – affectionately called this possibly on account of their peaks once having housed druid tree temples and spots for worshipping the goddess Isis, to whom the ancient Romans dedicated the city of Londinium (modern-day London).

This weekly visit was ostensibly to keep himself looking neat, and he used to remind me regularly that this was essential for a gentleman, especially during my unkempt teenage years. From the time I was seven up until that long-haired mystic phase, my grandfather would take me with him now and then as a special Saturday-morning treat, and Sid the Barber and I developed a fondness for each other.

The real show at the barber's shop was a sort of vaudevillian double act between Sid and Marge, the voluptuous, full-lipped, ridiculously provocative – some might say tarty – manicurist, with a supporting cast of whichever East End characters and villains were assembled at the time. Sid's part was to share his life wisdom, which was evidently great. Marge's was to mock him and make everyone laugh just as they were about to nod in agreement with the clipper-wielding sage.

I always reckon that barbers (and taxi drivers) are a good bet when you're in the market for some life wisdom. If I were the Tao and had to cast someone in the role of the archetypal wise barber, it would have to be Sid.

Built like a bulldog with a kindly face and gently smiling, twinkling eyes, he'd stand over me with the clippers and ask me rhetorical questions and then answer them himself: 'What do people want? Money and power.'

Marge would then chime in with a saucy wink: 'And a bit of the other . . .'

Everyone would chuckle and add their own quips. The first time I chuckled because they chuckled, although I couldn't see anything funny about 'the other'.

'What's "the other"?' I asked my grandfather on the way back.

He explained to me that when a couple was courting or in love, they'd 'canoodle' with each other, give each other 'a bit of a kiss and a cuddle'. That was what 'the other' was.

I still couldn't see what was so humorous about it but thought it was funny because *they* thought it was funny, so I chuckled again. I've never really changed my position on that. I still find English sexual innuendo gags totally unfunny and a symptom of a deeply repressed and sexually confused society.

After the first couple of times, Sid would seek a response from me. When he asked the question, I'd have to dutifully reply: 'Money and power . . . and a bit of the other.' For this, I'd earn an approving nod from Sid and a wink from Marge. She gave great winks.

The last time I visited Sid, I was 12 years old and moving from a 'mod' cut to a hippie noncut – out of his domain forever. He could tell, and treated me with a new kind of respect mixed with suspicion. Barbers were naturally in the front line in the battle against the then-burgeoning long-haired counterculture. Sid evidently felt threatened and somewhat betrayed that I was going over to the other side.

When he asked me the question, I answered rebelliously: 'Happiness. People want happiness.' And the whole room fell silent for a moment as each person there was forced to face the impossible conundrum that my statement presented them with.

This was somewhat revolutionary. These days, the pursuit of happiness is taken as a birthright, but back then the pursuit of happiness was for dreamers.

I still flip between the two and am never really sure what people really want most: money and power, or happiness. And maybe it doesn't matter. Ever since, I've been experimenting with and promoting the notion that a person can achieve both.

BIG DEREK

While on the theme of developing the instinctual street wisdom regarding what people want, Big Derek (so called because he was a big man in stature and presence) had a significant part to play in my education in terms of people skills. It was my first summer job. I was 14 and needed cash to pay for my escapades and explorations of the London underground scene. I was now held fully in thrall by it to the point of climbing in and out of my bedroom window to escape detection after curfew, which I usually managed to do. Only occasionally was I confronted by an angry father standing in my bedroom door as I hoisted a leg over the windowsill at 4 A.M., a little worse for wear.

I got myself a job selling fringed, suede Native American-style vest – we called them hippie waistcoats – for the grand sum of £3.10 each (which was about $7.50 US at 1968 exchange rates) at an indoor market on London's busy sacred shrine to consumerism: Oxford Street. I was on a basic salary of £4 a week plus 10 pence commission for each one I sold. You can hardly buy a bottle of water for that these days, but back then if I came home after a long six-day working week with £8 or £10 in my pocket, I could live like a king, give my mother a pound for good karma, and still save some for a rainy day.

Big D was my boss, and he was a tyrant. He was a burly former outdoor-market trader of the old school, tough as nails and supremely insulting, but very funny with it. It was hard, though, seeing the comedic side when his insults were directed at me, as they inevitably were a few times a day. The dislike I felt for him at the start gradually gave way to grudging admiration and eventually to love. And the funny thing was that the more I grew to love Big D, the less insulting he became.

One day, after watching me close my eighth sale before lunchtime – I was on a lucky roll – he called me over and invited me to stand with him at the cash register. This was akin to a knighthood.

'When you sell someone a waistcoat, what are they getting?' he asked.

'A waistcoat?' I replied cheekily.

He whacked me about the ear semi-playfully (it still hurt a bit). 'They're getting a moment of feeling good about themselves.'

This made an impact on my mind. I stopped being cheeky for a moment.

'That's your job – making people feel good about themselves. It doesn't matter what you're selling them. People want to feel good about themselves.'

I thought about this a lot, viewing it as an expansion of Sid the Barber's money and power theorem. Then, by putting it into action, I was pretty much instantly selling enough waistcoats to earn the princely sum of £14 a week. I was in the big time.

The day I left, Big Derek said, 'You're a salesman.' It was his way of paying me the highest accolade he knew.

I was aware that he meant it as an honour and thanked him, although inside I was thinking, *No, I'm fucking not.*

In retrospect, however, his ideas can be translated into the Taoist model, which holds that presentation skills when bringing your creative fruits to the public arena for the good of all, constitute one of the 'five excellences'. I realise now how Derek's crude, brutal, yet effective training has served me well during those phases where presenting myself and my creative output has been required. Additionally, and more importantly, it helped inform and confirm the subtext of all the work I've done since: to help people feel good about themselves. Fortunately, I've broadened my repertoire of tricks beyond selling fringed, suede hippie waistcoats, as that might have made for a more one-dimensional life than I'd have been willing to settle for. And you wouldn't be reading this book, or at least *I* wouldn't have written it.

DEAR DAPHNE

I love that name. Daphne. I only need to say it, and I'm
instantly transported to an alternative dimension. Some
years subsequent to the period in time with which this
book ends, I created a fragrance and developed it into
a highly successful range of body products. The project
fell apart through a few unforeseen, bizarre twists of fate.
However, it will be back soon – maybe even by the time
you read this – in an improved, all-natural form. The point,
though, is that as part of the life-enhancing repertoire of
this barefoot doctor, it all began with Daphne when I was
nine years old. I was at an all-boys boarding school in the
Chiltern Hills, way out in the countryside north of London
and starved of the female touch. One day I was sitting
on a bench in the great hall with my friend Julian when
Daphne, the French teacher's French wife, walked past us,
leaving a waft of fine fragrance in her wake.

'Mmm,' I vocalised.

'What?' asked Julian.

'Her perfume. Can you smell it?'

Julian rolled his eyes to heaven and made a noise of
disgust that I should be such an idiot to be moved by
something so soft and feminine. I remember thinking
what an idiot *he* was but said nothing. I figured even then,
when it comes to sensual appreciation, you've either got
it or you don't. And if you don't, no amount of persuasion
will change that.

I spent the next few decades chasing that scent until I actually made my own version of it, by then also influenced by a few other more earthly factors, but that's a subject for my autobiography. Here, I just want to give Daphne her place in the scheme of things and put it forth as an example of how someone can change another person's life simply by walking by and wafting a fragrance.

You just never know the effect you'll have on others when you step out of the house in the morning.

*** ***

Chapter Four

Opening Up to Whom I Was Becoming

I'm going to whisk us along a bit here: teenage years spent in the haze of school exams, girls, dancing, hitchhiking through Europe, being a runner for a gangster called Curly Diamonds (also one for the autobiography), and exploring the more materialistic side of life. Then one day, Stephen, a rich hippie friend of mine (who had the best physique in the universe) showed me the warrior pose – a particular pose of hatha yoga, which he'd just started learning. He looked good doing it, and I wanted to look like that too. So with that profound motivation (profoundly vain), I went along to his yoga class. It was taught by one of the most remarkable people I've ever met.

JOHNNY STIRK

These days, Johnny Stirk is one of the world's most internationally respected yoga teachers. Back then he was just plain crazy in his zeal to get people to loosen up. He'd actually stand on my legs with his full body weight as I sat in tailor's pose (a seated position, with the soles of your feet touching and knees pressed downward), or stand on my lower back when I was in child's posture (seated on your knees, as you lay your torso on your thighs, hands placed alongside your body, palms up). I guess I was crazy to let him, but the high of the extreme stretch – we'd hold each asana (yogic pose) for at least ten minutes – was so stupendous that it was worth every bit of pain (and even the occasional bad lower back I've suffered from periodically ever since). I take full responsibility for it, though – I could have said no.

Today there are enough unscrupulous, litigation-happy characters around who'd sue, and a guy like Johnny could and would never teach like that now. That's a shame, in a way. Although the body's structure might have been somewhat strained by such extreme practices, the ensuing enlightenment and rapid opening of the entire mind-body-spirit complex made that a small price to pay.

Johnny would stand on top of me while insisting: 'Breathe, just breathe; come on, breathe.' As I trembled like a crazy horse and my muscles let go, he taught me one of the most invaluable lessons of my life: if you surrender to pain and breathe through it, it will not only pass more swiftly, but you'll also experience a massive expansion in yourself on all levels as a result. And this subsequently translates into an expansion of your good fortune in life.

PETER WALKER

Married at the time to Jeb, whom I'll tell you about later on, Peter Walker was and is one of the world's great characters. The first time I met him I was entranced by his spirit. I'd never met anyone with a more expressive face or with such a delighted twinkle in his eyes, which remained even as he somehow accommodated all the pain and suffering of humanity.

He was sitting at a table in the living room of his flat in the Little Venice area of London writing (by hand) the first of a whole slew of books about baby massage and baby gymnastics. He's now a global titan in this field . . . if there's such a thing as a *titan* in the world of baby massage and gymnastics.

I say that he was writing a book, but judging by the huge amount of crumpled-up pieces of paper pretty much covering the floor of the room, he was doing far more crumpling than writing. Peter possessed a natural expertise on the topic. He was evidently so in touch with, and expressive of, his own inner child that he was able to naturally resonate with babies and children of all ages. He'd generally be found with gaggles of children hanging off his legs and arms performing various somersaults and rolls about his person.

During our first conversation, he read to me from the Gospel of Thomas, a rare book back then. Specifically, he read the part about how one must speak with a newborn baby in order to know divine wisdom. This implies that infants have come through from the sacred realm more recently than anyone else and so are still freshly imbued with such knowledge.

In any case, it was Peter's visible respect for all people, and especially babies, that taught me how all of us are children; and that all of our pretending to be adults is really just a game for babies, metaphorically speaking.

To be yourself, you have to be the child within you. The only thing that happens when you grow older is that you hopefully learn to behave more harmoniously with yourself and others.

Peter's influence deeply affected the way I've behaved as a father. It also taught me to exercise the same nurturing paternal energy I have with my sons with everyone I meet. It's the most viable form that I know of for expressing universal love. Peter also influenced or rather somehow gave permission for me to adapt Taoist massage routines to use on babies and teach this to thousands of parents all over the world. I did so under the guidance of Yehudi Gordon, the renowned obstetrician who became infamous in the '70s for being the first medical doctor in the UK to champion natural childbirth. They were so into stirrups and epidurals back then that Dr. Gordon was actually expelled from the National Health Service. (I'll tell you more about him later, as he also played a pivotal role in my training.)

I don't really have any startling stories about Peter, other than that even today his fascination for his life-work remains, which for me is admirable. Although I love people and find babies irresistible in general, there's only so much baby reality I can take without going a bit 'gloopy' in the brain. Meantime, Peter still flies around the globe from Byron Bay to Birmingham, teaching parents and midwives his art while maintaining a childlike wonder and innocence even in his mid-60s.

JOHN KELLS

The first time I saw people doing tai chi was an odd experience for me. I'd never seen it in my life before – not many Westerners had in those days. Yet I recognised it instantly as if I'd always been familiar with it. I somehow knew exactly what it was, what it was for, and what it could do – it was the dance of power, the spirit dance, the warrior flying on land – but I'd never actually seen or heard of it until then.

So there I am, wandering through Regents Park in London, a place I've gravitated to at many key points in my life. The ground there has some sort of special energy for me. Many of my life-changing experiences have occurred at the park, and this one turns out to be right up there in the top regions of the list.

Two guys with ponytails are engaging in what I now know to be the Yang-style tai chi long form in perfect unison, about 30 feet apart. I know they're American. This is the mid-1970s, and ponytails are an exclusively American hippie thing in London at that time.

I'm instantly entranced and transfixed, as much by the anomaly of knowing what they're doing without knowing what they're doing. It's as if there are two of me at the same time. I squat down yoga-style at a respectful distance to enter more fully into the spirit of the anomalous moment, and to watch until they finish. Except they don't finish. These two guys with ponytails just keep doing it and doing it . . . and I eventually have to get home.

On the way, I drop in to see Johnny Stirk. 'What's that thing they do – you know, the slow-dance thing where they wave their arms about like feathers?'

'Feathers? Do you mean tai chi?'

'Think so.' It struck a chord. 'Like slow-motion karate.'

'Yeah, that's tai chi.'

'I've got to learn that. Who teaches it? Where can I go?'

He tells me about Gary Wragg, the famous artist who practises it every morning in the communal garden we all live by, and suggests that I ask him.

So I get up early the next day, and at 7 A.M. I'm standing in the cold waiting for Gary Wragg to appear, which he duly does, as if out of the mist. He bows subtly and says, 'Hello, how can I help you?'

I explain that I want to learn tai chi and was wondering if he can recommend anyone to teach me. He tells me to come to the school he goes to: Grandmaster Chi's school. (I still can't hear mention of Grandmaster Flash without instantly combining him and Grandmaster Chi to comedic effect in my imagination.) Well, that sounds good enough to me, so I show up, having already gotten a pair of tai chi slippers, the black cotton ones with the brown plastic soles, perfect for spinning on the balls of your feet.

Strangely enough, it was while trying on those slippers in Chinatown that I first had the realisation that China would be the world's next big empire. *It starts with the shoes,* I thought, *and they work upward and outward from there.* I imagined that the Chinese had perhaps inserted some sort of psychic coding in the soles that worked its way in through your feet up to your head, and then you'd be brainwashed and under control. I even recall wondering if I could write a novel about it, but figured George Orwell had already done the definitive version . . . so what was the point? In my life, I've only been interested in being an original.

So there I am, standing with 20 or so others – mostly hippie-like folk – in this mirrored basement, wearing my Chinese slippers (and hoping the 'code' wasn't seeping into me too much). The shadowy figure of Grandmaster Chi/Flash hovers just out of peripheral vision. The main teacher, John Kells, in his black cotton, white mandarin-collar tai chi pyjama suit, is talking about how tai chi is a martial art in which we use our opponents' force rather than our own to overcome them.

For me, it's first day of aikido, take two. And it's how tai chi uses *chi* (*ki*) to move the opponent and how *chi* promotes good health. And how *chi* is the Tao in motion. I'm familiar with the concept of the 'Tao' but have never thought much about it. Thinking about it as I stand there brings me an instant feeling of all-over warmth and comfort in my skin. I've arrived back home: a home I left lifetimes ago but to which I've returned. I'm relieved. I'm also aware that this aspect of me that has just arrived is not my usual self. I'm watching the tussle going on between that everyday self and this older aspect, and I'm glad to note that this aspect isn't willing to let my everyday self spoil its enjoyment of this homecoming moment.

As I'm processing all this, John is talking about how the *chi* is issued from the *tan t'ien* below the navel, which I'm linking with the 'one point' (the *hara* or *tanden* of aikido). He's talking about moving from this centre as a unified entity and that when you do, you're unstoppable.

He then calls Gary The Famous Artist over – he's also wearing the tai chi pyjamas – and demonstrates how, when Gary throws a hefty punch his way, he's able to neutralise it and throw Gary clean across the room with hardly more than a feather's worth of pressure.

I laugh. It's funny. Both Gary and John laugh too, and then everyone laughs. This is different from what I'm used to—in aikido, no one ever laughed. I'm feeling elated and seeing how all the aikido training was so perfect. How I'd needed that sort of tough discipline to learn self-discipline, which after all is the cornerstone of any spiritual or psycho-physical discipline. But that now I've graduated to the adult level, where people are able to laugh like humans in the midst of a training session. This is sophisticated.

I'm high on appreciating what's going on. ·

We start the warm-up exercises without a word being said, without a command being shouted; we simply fall in behind John. The warm-up is all about getting your body to soften up and unify itself around your navel area to get the *chi* to flow in your channels and generally grant you optimal levels of personal power.

Again, I'm totally familiar with every single exercise, but have never actually seen or felt anything like them in my life before.

Then we begin the forms, and I'm flying through them without hesitation. The *chi* is literally coursing through me. I'm enveloped in invisible, thick-pile velvet. Yet even so, my everyday mind is going on and on about how fucking weird it all is.

And I'm still enjoying this internal theatre and starting to marvel at how easy it is for me to do the postures and make the moves even though my muscles and joints are feeling a bit strange being this soft. In aikido, the muscles and sinews were more externally taut. I've never seen or felt softness like this.

Then we 'push hands'. Pushing hands is a formalised style of slow-motion boxing for two people and has to be one of the most fascinating, riveting games in the universe when you're in the mood for it. It requires no strength other than to remain standing, and relies entirely on intelligence, both in the way you feel into the opponent's energy and the way you stack your bones up in the correct alignment to take advantage of body mechanics – in order to issue the *chi* from your legs, through your waist, up your back, down your arms and out through your palms.

And there's this other part of me that simply wants to get out of there and be frivolous and superficial. But I know it's impossible – once I've started, there's no turning back. I know this incontrovertibly: I cannot turn back now. I've woken up a memory of a former self from another lifetime. The Japanese phase of learning aikido was just preparing me for this one: the real coming home. Yet it still gives me the creeps a bit . . . nice creeps, though.

I owe a lot to John Kells, Gary Wragg, and all the members of the Grandmaster Chi/Flash crew, who got me started on the Taoism path, which provided the blueprint for everything that followed. In addition, they initiated my ongoing enquiry into the unparalleled way its medicine and alchemy work in respect to body, mind, and spirit health, as well as all aspects of life from the creative to the financial.

Taoism also offered me repeated proof that things could happen before my very eyes, and I had to struggle to believe them even though I'd just seen them happen (or had I?), which was simply because my concept of reality was at odds with reality itself. This is also a major theme underscoring all the work I do: pointing out that our concept of reality isn't sacred and is merely a construct susceptible to transformation, by which actual reality will transform in turn.

Every now and then in class we'd engage in intensive sessions to explore the power of *chi*. Someone would stand five or six feet away from you with his eyes closed. You'd hold your palms up, facing toward him, and start moving your hands slowly, projecting your *chi* at him. He would have no idea what you were doing but would soon start moving with your hands as if by remote control.

John liked pushing hands with me. It was probably the aikido he felt in me. By hardly touching me, he was able to totally grab hold of my mind and hurl me across the room, which was like flying. I love flying. Always have. I used to fly almost every night in my dreams as a kid, and I still often do. I've perfected my stroke and can hover above the ground or soar way above the clouds at will (in my dreams). I love flying in planes; I love whizzing through the air. I was probably once a big bird myself. Yehudi Gordon always called me that. I seem to remember my big-bird life so clearly when I'm dreaming . . . so I loved being hurled across the room. I'd giggle my head off every time.

I trained with great diligence to learn the art of doing that but got nowhere fast. It requires a lifetime of study. I met up with John again recently (by divinely ordained serendipity) and witnessed that he has perfected the art. He doesn't even have to make a physical gesture of a push; he can do it entirely with his intention. He doesn't even have to wiggle his nose. He just exhales and you go flying.

John has been teaching me how to achieve this. One day I managed to lift a man (who was larger than me) clean off the floor by an inch or so without using an ounce of strength. My rational mind still can't accept this, but I'm digressing into the recent past. Let's get back to the deep past.

When it was time for me to leave for New Mexico in 1979, I spent some time sitting with John. He was moved by my adventurous spirit and was incredibly supportive even though he didn't want to lose me as a student. He wrote something on a piece of paper, folded it, and told me to read it and promise to do what it said. He said that it was the only thing I needed to know in the whole world to keep me safe.

I promised even though I hadn't seen what he'd written.

When I got outside, I opened the note. It stated: 'Do one hour of practice every single day. If you miss a day, make up for it the next.' The humble simplicity of it made me cry a bit right there in the street.

I've stuck to it ever since, with the addition of the two other Taoist martial arts I was to learn a bit later in America. And he was right on the mark. It works.

*** ***

Chapter Five

No Turning Back Now

I'm walking along Chung Kong Road in Hong Kong one Sunday afternoon in my late teens feeling a bit disoriented on the first day of my first visit to the Far East. I'm on a spiritual tourist trip and vaguely wondering where I'm going to find myself a master of Taoism. Being relatively tall and fair for these parts, my head is sticking out like a sore thumb over a mass of dark, bobbing heads, which is all I can see before me on the teeming street. I'm feeling jet-lagged and sweaty, my nose rebelling against the musty smell of humidity mixed with spices and the outflow of a million air-conditioning units, and wondering if I'm mad for being here in the first place. I'm wondering, too, as I often do, whether this compulsive wanderlust of mine is a good thing; and I'm probably looking a bit existentially lost.

I walk up to a shop window to check out the technology display. It's the mid-1970s, so it's all calculators and personal cassette players. I don't want anything. I just need to change the view and focus on something other than this mass of moving heads below me. The boy in me is trying to get his bearings by focusing on familiar gadgets to find some reference points. I'm undergoing intense culture recalibration. I wouldn't say shock; but I'm of half a mind to get straight back on a plane and escape to India, Australia, or anywhere else with a more familiar feel about it.

The other half of my mind is just telling me to stop and relax, as there will surely be a jewel in this expedition if only I have the patience and guts to stay with it. The ability to override the urge to escape at every turn from whatever adventure I've set myself up for by talking to myself (rather than giving way to panic) is something I've learned, along with all other facets of self-discipline, from Tio. I'm finding by now that when all else fails, it's mostly the meditation technique he taught me that settles me back into the ride.

So here I am, in the midst of this busy shopping area, touching the tip of my second finger to the tip of my thumb on both hands to calm and re-centre myself, just as Tio always taught. It's a technique that sends the *chi* down and back up the arms, then into the chest, from where it drops into the *hara* or *tan t'ien* (lower abdominal region below the navel). This helps my whole body and mind settle, as I breathe slowly to make my *chi* circulate more strongly. I'm wondering whether if I continue, rather than indulging in feeling glum and displaced, I'll be mysteriously drawn to whichever Taoist master I'm destined to meet. This has been the reason for my expedition to Hong Kong in the first place.

I've done well. I have a good job and place to stay, and am reminding myself of this and just retrieving my positive spirit, when I notice someone standing next to me, who's also staring into the shop window. Or rather he isn't staring at the display; he's staring at me, looking at my hands and giggling.

THE BEAUTEOUS MASTER

I turn to my left and there's this guy who looks about my age, but who actually turns out to be in his mid-40s, smiling at me with the most compassionate expression I've ever seen. In fact, as I stand there, I realise that until that moment I've never actually seen compassion in real life. If you can imagine all the kindness ever experienced or expressed by all the people in the world since time began, and then imagine that funnelled through one face and one set of smiling eyes, it still wouldn't quite give you the picture of how utterly compassionate this person is. His face is as clear as a still, pristine lake. It's instantly evident that there is absolutely nothing sinister or self-serving about him. There's not a single shadow in his eyes – he's pure compassion in motion.

I can describe the experience now in retrospect, but standing there at the time, it isn't an intellectual experience – it's a visceral sensation. I'm flooded with instant love and overwhelmed by a sensation of his kindness penetrating every cell of my body.

'Do you need some help?' he asks.

'Do you work in this shop?' I respond. This sends him into peals of giggles.

'No, I don't work in this shop. Where are you from?'

'London.'

This sets him off again. I don't really know what's so funny. Perhaps it's just the ultimate joke of how we all rush around the planet looking for things that are usually in our own backyards; of how we all take ourselves and our adventures so deadly seriously when ultimately none of it matters, as we're all going to die anyway. But it doesn't matter what the joke is. I start giggling too, and we fall into a full-blown spontaneous giggling session right there on that busy street of a million moving head-tops.

We introduce ourselves. His name is William. I remember thinking it's a funny name for a Chinese guy and being thankful he has an English name. It makes me feel safer. I even remember thinking how funny it is to be reassured by things like that.

'What are you doing here?' he asks.

'I want to learn about Taoism,' I mumble, embarrassed.

'No, I mean, what are you doing on Chung Kong Road?'

More giggles between us.

'I don't know. I was just walking to get my bearings. I was looking around.'

He invites me to his family home in Kowloon. We walk through Kowloon Park, where people are doing tai chi and dancing the foxtrot under the trees.

'Tai chi, ballroom,' he says and giggles as if everything in the world is a joke.

'Yes. I'm learning tai chi,' I tell him. 'I've never learned how to foxtrot, although I do like to waltz. You know the waltz?' I parody a few steps as we walk along, my arm out holding an imaginary partner.

'Yes, yes, waltz, very good,' and he cracks up again and does a few parody steps of his own. I'm giggling because I'm totally overwhelmed by everything and am not sure if I love it all or hate it all. I haven't fully understood yet that I can do both at the same time, and that's okay.

We walk along Austin Road, and I'm saying the name over and over in my head for some reason: *Austin, Austin, Austin*. It makes me feel safe thinking about Austin Motor Co., but I also just like repeating the word for the sound, as if it has significance.

I'm talking to William about aikido and why I'd been pressing my fingers to my thumbs. I'm feeling overwhelmed. The Chinese graphics everywhere, the intense concentration of gaudy colours, the indigo dye that has spilled out from the denim factories onto the road surface, the noise, the old men gambling on the traffic islands and sitting in vacant parking lots; and the mad, claustrophobic, spice-scented, musty crowdedness of it all is starting to make me feel nauseated in an 'I want my mummy' sort of way.

I'm explaining this to William as he leads me through the maze of backstreets (with me also wondering how the fuck I'm ever going to remember my way back, and trying to leave an imaginary trail of breadcrumbs in my mind).

We arrive at his apartment, and he introduces me to his wife and 17-year-old utterly beautiful, like-out-of-a-Chinese-fairy-tale daughter. She and I instantly get caught in a mutual game of eyeballs, and I fall hopelessly in love. I say *hopelessly* because even at that tender age, I can see that there's a vast gulf between the romantic and the real. There's no way I'll be able to pull this one off under the circumstances, and it's going nowhere even before it begins. This doesn't stop the game of eyeballs, however.

William's wife is the pragmatic one who keeps it all together. She's the boss. And he's fine with that. There's an air of harmony in that household that I've never encountered before and have never encountered since. I still hold it up as my one and only true example of how

a relationship between a man and woman can actually
work.

William asks if I want to see his private room, his
temple.

Thinking that this is probably normal and that
everyone has a private temple in their home in Hong
Kong, I take it all in my stride. However, the icons are
unfamiliar and the tiny room has a palpable atmosphere
of being imbued with a mystical presence – perhaps with
invisible beings, spirits, or angels. I don't know . . . but I
can feel something in the room.

William looks at my face and giggles again. 'Spirits,
ancestors.'

'Are you a Taoist?' I ask.

He giggles a bit more. 'In Hong Kong, Taoism,
Buddhism – the ancestors all the same, all mixed
together.' He makes a mixing-bowl gesture. I'm a
little disappointed to hear this, as I've built up a purist
fantasy about Taoism. Still, I realise how fortunate I am
to be introduced to the way things really are, rather than
being subjected to a second-hand, idealised, packaged
version for Western consumption. Further, how absurdly
fortunate – but that's how it's always seemed to work
for me – it is for me to meet the very person I want
to meet, as if it's ordained. And how fortunate it is
that he's unmistakably kind and compassionate. I've
always assumed Taoist masters would be serious sons of
bitches.

He shows me around his artefacts. The centrepiece is a three-tiered jade structure in the stylised shape of someone sitting in meditation. It consists of three small deities sitting one on top of the other, in the belly, chest, and head regions, respectively. They have serene, all-knowing expressions. In front of this, a small clump of sweet-and-sour fragranced incense sticks is burning, unlike the Indian variety I'm familiar with. On the walls are all sorts of calligraphic images: talismans to bring about good fortune, health, and harmony; to keep flies away; and so on.

The walls are a dark blue, similar to the indigo dye on the streets. I remember wondering if he used indigo dye to paint the walls.

I just stand there saying, 'Wow,' over and over like a stunned idiot, not knowing what else to say. Although it's all unfamiliar – I've never seen any Taoist iconography before and have never considered the whole notion of being in touch with one's ancestors – I feel incredibly comfortable and at ease. It's as if I've grown up around such things and am totally at home with them. I'm sure this is something I've brought through with me to this lifetime. I feel it but at that time I'm not yet in the habit of fully formulating thoughts like that. That level of insight hasn't woken up in me completely; for now, it just feels right, all the way through my body. I'm keenly aware of how relaxed I am with this stranger, whom I already feel I've known all my life.

'Will you teach me?'

'Of course,' he replies with much kindness. All my misgivings about the trip, all the overwhelming unfamiliar smells, the humidity, the garish neon, the noise, the disorientation, the jet lag, the existential unrest and the displacement sensation evaporate in his smile.

'What would you like to learn?'

Part of me wants to say, 'To be like you so I can marry your daughter and live happily ever after in some fairy-tale land where cultural divides don't exist, and not being able to speak the same language or share any familiar reference points doesn't matter.' But instead I get pragmatic and say, 'To do magic. I want to be a magician. I don't mean a conjurer. I want to understand how reality works – I want to understand how the world works.'

Reading this today it may sound a bit strange. Now, everyone thinks they know everything about everything on account of the Internet. But back then there were few books about these topics, and they weren't readily available. At best, the whole escapade of training myself to become a man of knowledge was a stumble in the dark. It was really hard finding out what I needed to know, to discover what all the various disciplines were called and what each comprised, and hard to find out how they all corresponded. It was virtually virgin territory, which is why it was so exciting (and that's something I fear is missing from the quest these days). Now it's all packaged and marketed.

William giggles again, as if he's been reading my mind about his daughter. Indeed, I've actually been feeling something running interference on my thoughts all the while, a voice of unusual reason pointing out the futility of indulging the fantasy. I'm sure it's his voice. It's as if he's looking into my soul and understanding, with utmost compassion, how confusing reality and the world is for me yet how small a shift of perspective would be needed to undo that mind-set. And further, making that small shift would take me years and decades. I'm saying this in retrospect, for at the time I'm just feeling all this to be so, and am not formulating it into thoughts. I just know why he's laughing and the joke is huge in its implications.

'There is no magic. It's all just Tao,' he says.

We arrange for me to come over for tea another day and fall into a pattern of me visiting a couple of times a week. We talk and drink tea in the living room. I gaze into his daughter's eyes for a while, thinking William isn't noticing but knowing that he is. His wife is definitely noticing, but she seems to like it for some reason. It amuses her. After pleasantries and tea and conversation about how tough or otherwise gentle life has been this week, William and I retire to the tiny temple room and gradually, as the weeks go by, he shows me bits and pieces of Taoist rituals. They involve uttering strange screeching sounds, like a quietly screaming banshee, while making bizarre hand and arm gestures, shaking rattles, and ringing bells . . . but all done with good humour, albeit with extreme intent.

William isn't teaching me so much as sharing with me. I'm not intending to learn the rituals specifically. I'm not a buff like that. I just want the nuts of it, the gist, so I can adapt it to work for me. I'm not one to have an identity crisis, as do some when they embark on a discipline originated by a different culture. I know I'm not Chinese and don't want to be. I just want to learn their magic. I already understand that the roots of all spiritual paths are universal.

William understands this relative crudeness of approach to the great mysteries and respects my natural Western pragmatism. It fascinates him. To him, I'm a semi-cultured caveman. He doesn't judge me; he loves me for it. He's not strict about conducting the rituals and has no superstition that requires me to act with reverence, which is handy as I'm compulsively drawn to crack any and every gag as opportunity arises. Everything makes him chuckle, and if he forgets and grows serious for a moment while we sit drinking tea or eating noodles, his wife reminds him by telling him off for something or other, which makes him laugh.

But with all his good humour and emotional suppleness he clearly knows how to channel the *chi* and direct his intention with great potency. He does magic for me; three rituals to set me off on the fabulous global adventure I tell him I want, and I feel the power in it. My facial hairs stand on end and the back of my neck shudders. I also note that my temperature rises, and I'm sweating more than usual in the oppressive humidity. I feel as if I'm surrounded by a presence that he's summoned into the room – a fairy godfather who will take care of me as I go. It's visceral, and has nothing to do with imagination or wanting to feel something to please William.

He doesn't care anyway. For him, everything is perfect as it is and everyone is complete as they are. That's the basis of the magic. You have to know that everything is as it's meant to be and that's perfect. You're not actually attempting to change reality. You show reality utmost respect by honouring it as it is. Then with all the *chi* you can summon to support yourself, you envision it differently and in the fullness of time, it changes for you – but you don't change it. This process, or rather non-process (because you are not doing, you are allowing), is usually described as *wu-wei,* or non-action.

None of this is spoken or explained intellectually. I'm reading a translation of Lao-tzu's *Tao Te Ching,* the so-called bible of Taoism, so I'm able to understand the premise, but otherwise I observe. I feel. I experience. I evaluate, although evaluation is merely an indulgence. I see things I don't believe with my eyes, even though I'm seeing them. None of that matters, as it's just stuff of the mind. What matters is being present.

And what matters most about being present, more than all the understanding, wisdom, or power, is exercising compassion: for oneself, for the other, for all others, for life itself. Compassion is the key to eventually unlock every mystery. And realising that all mysteries have already been unlocked is the way to unlock them.

It doesn't make sense to the rational mind.

But then neither does the sight of the people I'm looking at from William's window: old men totally focused on gambling while sitting on traffic islands as cars and trucks rush by either side of them. It doesn't have to make sense to the rational mind. I grapple with this but finally can't be bothered to expend the energy. It's too humid to make the effort.

In any case, these tiny temple interludes are really just a way for William and me to pass the time together. Teaching me his magic is simply the game we play together as two friends: the refined master from this ancient and highly evolved culture and the hairy Western barbarian. The real transmission and learning received from William, beauteous master, is his compassion, compared to which gaining dexterity and power from learning a million magic rituals is merely a trinket in spiritual terms.

To this day, when I have to remind myself to exercise compassion, it's William's smile and the feeling of warmth that would flood me in his presence that I use as my model and trigger.

VENERABLE GESHE

Venerable Geshe, a Tibetan Buddhist master, would come to the tai chi school once a month to conduct a meditation session with all the students. The fact that two disciplines could work in harmony together and not clash was in itself educational and mind-expanding. Especially since they weren't scrunched into some hybrid form called *TaoBudd* or *Buddtao,* or some other awful-sounding trademarked name, and taught in suburban health clubs and on morning TV shows as the latest wellbeing scam (as might be the case today).

Nothing was ever said about it. No one remarked on how unusual it was. People didn't compartmentalise reality so much in those days. It was simply accepted.

Geshe looked about 17 but was probably around 60. He'd been in monasteries since the age of six and evidently saw through the illusion of everyday life so clearly all he could do was chuckle. He chuckled fairly consistently, unless he was meditating. He couldn't speak English, at least not very much, so chuckling also served to bridge the communication gap.

He'd walk in and sit in an armchair that had been brought in and placed in a corner of the tai chi dojo and would chuckle as everyone sat down on the floor. Then without a word of instruction, he'd stop chuckling and close his eyes.

Everyone would close their eyes and fall silent. Then a remarkable thing would happen – and I checked with other people afterwards to determine if I was blowing things out of proportion (and I wasn't). My mind, the inside of my brain, would instantly become flooded with light. I'm not talking metaphorically. I wasn't sitting there visualising or imagining light. It was as if someone had installed a 60-watt halogen bulb under my crown and turned it on.

When Geshe meditated, his consciousness was so clear and unfettered by the shadows of illusion or self-importance that it emitted an actual light that would infiltrate and fill the minds of those who were present. I don't think he actively transmitted it. So immersed in simply being, he wasn't doing anything.

Once a month we sat like that for an hour, basking in the light and thinking nothing, for this light was so strong it cleansed the mind of thoughts without us having to try. Even the usual familiar debate and commentary in the front of my brain (about how amazing it was to have my brain flooded with light like this) would stop.

Having learned to meditate from the age of 11 and understanding how hard it is to reach this hallowed state of pure consciousness, I realised how privileged I was to be in the room with him and everyone present. It was patently clear during these sessions that earthly pursuits – no matter how seemingly grand or important, and even including missions to save or heal the world – were insignificant in reality, and that experiencing the pure light of consciousness was the only experience worth pursuing.

As soon as Geshe opened his eyes, everyone seemed to feel it at the same time. The whole room would come to simultaneously, without a word being said or the meditation bell being sounded. I would return, as if obliged, to the movie in my forebrain: it concerned some Superman-like drive to save and heal the world, and that mission involved lists of things to do. I still have lists of things to do every day but am no longer concerned with saving the world. The world will either save and heal itself, or it won't. My only concern these days is to contribute value and leave the rest to the Tao: what will be, will be. But back then, I was driven by ambition and a growing missionary zeal. So I'd come to awareness, having just experienced the divine nectar, and would instantly snap back into internal agenda-driven mode.

At the end, we'd file past Geshe to shake his hand (softly) and say thank you. He'd just sit with his legs crossed under his robes on that armchair, chuckling. I'd invariably give him a kiss on the cheek because he was simply so lovely he deserved it. He always seemed to chuckle a bit more when I walked up, as if he knew and understood the paradox occurring within me.

When it came time for me to leave for America in 1979, I attended that month's session with a heavy heart. I'd miss Geshe. He had no idea I was leaving – he had never uttered a word to me in more than two years. All he'd done was chuckle a lot at me, and all I'd ever said was, 'Hi, Geshe.'

However, at the end of that last session, when I filed past and gave him the customary kiss on the cheek, he held my hand to stop me, and said compassionately and softly so no one else could hear, 'You must lead a spiritual life.'

'I know, Geshe, but I have things to do first.'

He chuckled properly at this. 'You must lead a spiritual life; otherwise, you waste your time.' At that he held my hand and looked deeply and surprisingly seriously into my eyes.

'I will one day, I promise,' I said with my cheekiest grin, kissed him again, and left.

I naturally rolled that exchange around in my mind for years afterwards until one day it finally clicked and I understood. The point was to spiritualise the everyday, and thus be in a state of enlightenment as I work, rest and play. Through all the books I've written and all the books they've inspired and have been inspired by, living in the everyday world in a meditative state seems quite ordinary these days. But back then, things were more separated. Blending the two to produce spirituality on the run was a groundbreaking move.

And it was Geshe who got me there, which is why I've blessed him every day since.

*** ***

Chapter Six

Ronnie, King of the World

When I met R. D. Laing ('Ronnie'), he was already king of his world. He was 50. I was 20. He reckoned that at 50 you become king (or presumably, queen – he never said) of your world; and he remains the clearest, most startling example of this maxim that I've ever encountered. In fact, he remains the clearest, most startling example of pretty much *every* quality and aspect I respect and admire in the human spirit.

What follows may appear hyperbolic, but be assured that I'm not about to gush. If anything, I'm playing it down. Let that be a gauge of my levels of respect and admiration for this giant of the psychic realms.

You might think that at 20, I would have been naturally in awe of any self-realised adult (no matter whether he or she was a captain of industry, musical hero, or doctor of the psyche) – but, in fact, I was already quite a cynical young bastard by then. I grew up in London and had encountered enough con artists not to be easily impressed. It would require true genius of any kind in any sphere to overcome that cynicism.

However, cynicism didn't even come close with Ronnie.

I find it intriguing that, especially after his death, he became extremely unpopular among the establishment – even by those who'd never met him. He was a maverick of the highest order, and many of his peers were envious of his ability to heal people rather than fudge it with drugs or electroshock treatments. There can be no other explanation, because without a doubt, Ronnie was one of the greatest healers and men ever to walk the earth.

While William, the beauteous master, was compassion personified, Ronnie was compassion in action, right there on the front line of human suffering.

Johnny Stirk, my yoga teacher, was a close friend of his and used to go on about how Ronnie says this and Ronnie says that, but I didn't know who he was talking about. 'Who's this Ronnie?' I asked one day, my curiosity sufficiently aroused.

'Here. Read this.' Johnny handed me a copy of *Politics of Experience*.

On a whim, I went down to Surrey and checked into
a hotel on a lake and read the book the whole weekend.
It wasn't easy. It was so compressed with knowledge that
digesting each paragraph was like opening up a zip file.

My mind felt as if it were becoming exponentially
wider, deeper, broader and higher via a series of
explosions of consciousness. It took ages to read and
reread each paragraph until the explosions came.

I sat on the bed, overlooking the lake, turning pages all
day and night; and by the end of the weekend, I'd finished
the book and was in a state of euphoria.

At last, someone who truly understood me: who
understood the sense of alienation, the bewilderment over
people's games . . . everything that had been tripping me
up since I was old enough to think. And Ronnie got it in
enough depth that just reading his words could radically
shift one's psycho-tectonic plates. It certainly did mine.

I've got to study with this man, I thought. *I will study
with this man,* I vowed. I just saw it. It was going to
happen. The fact that he was a psychotherapist was
irrelevant. He could have been a car mechanic – it
wouldn't have mattered. I wanted that wisdom, no matter
which form it was expressed through. I didn't want to be
a psychotherapist (and never did become one): sitting
around all day just talking and listening to one person after
another simply isn't my thing. I don't have the patience.

'I've got to meet him,' I said to Johnny. So he arranged
it.

There I was at 2 Eton Road, Belsize Park, North London, at 2 P.M. one Tuesday afternoon, sitting in the waiting area chatting chirpy 20-year-old nervous, flirty rubbish with his lovely secretary, Margarita, who actually wound up being Ronnie's partner before his death. And then the door to his study opened and a patient walked out, sheepishly avoiding my eyes. He was evidently in a hugely disturbed state, although somehow seemed settled by the session. I gleaned all this from his body language and my intuition, a faculty fairly well honed by years of aikido and, more recently, tai chi.

Suddenly I realise where I am and what I'm doing and feel ashamed of myself for conning my way in to see Ronnie by masquerading as someone in need of help. I'm thinking this as his head pops around the door, and he looks up diagonally at me with his left eyebrow raised in curiosity. I'm in love. I don't mean sexually or romantically. I mean existentially, in love with all my heart, soul and mind with this being who's radiating something I've never encountered before. I can't put my finger on it; I just love it and am aware of this. It helps me overcome my nerves and fraudulent feeling enough to follow his gesture into the room.

Ronnie sits down in his armchair, a cigarette burning in the ashtray, which makes it nice and informal; human rather than clinical.

He mumbles about me sitting wherever I want and gestures toward a couch to the side or an armchair

opposite him. I'm not going to lie down for this one
– I have to remain upright. This is the most important
moment of my life so far, and I know that clearly. It's as
if everything depends on it, yet I feel deceitful because
he's assuming I'm there because I'm not well. As far as
I'm concerned, in my unbelievably innocent way, I have
absolutely nothing wrong with me.

'I feel like a fraud being here—' I start.

His raises his left eyebrow quizzically again.

'. . . because there's nothing actually wrong with me.'

He laughs. 'Wouldn't you say that's quite a paradox?'
he asks, his instantly entrancing and reassuring Scottish
street accent hinting at irony.

'What?'

'Feeling fraudulent and there being nothing wrong
with you.'

That's a bit subtle for me at that stage.

'No, I mean, I haven't come for therapy. I've come here
because I want you to teach me.'

He looks at me with both eyebrows level for a
moment, probably summing up whether I'm indeed okay
and wanting to learn something, or in fact am seriously
messed up and have come to therapy with this I'm-not-
mad ruse as my opening gambit. I feel flattered when he's
evidently given my sanity the benefit of the doubt.

'I don't teach psychotherapy anymore. If you want
to learn to be a therapist, you can get in touch with the
Philadelphia Association.' (This was the body he headed up.)

'No, you don't understand. I don't want to learn psychotherapy. I don't want to be a therapist. I want to learn your wisdom.'

And I just sit there blushing and sweating, while he sits there looking at me extremely calmly, one eyebrow raised again, for what seems like three months.

'Okay,' he says, and smiles.

'Wow!' I blurt and go blank for a moment. 'What will we do? How will we do it? How much will you charge me?' I'm suddenly excited, neurotic and all over the place wanting to plan it out.

'I don't know. Tell me about yourself and why you want to learn to be wise.'

I sit talking a million miles an hour. I only get to the first day of boarding school when I was eight, and how it was impossible to cry when I said goodbye to my mum at the huge double doors of the school building because none of the other boys wanted to cry either and how I'd bottled it so effectively that I hadn't been able to cry properly since. 'That's something we could work on, I suppose,' I say, as if offering him a concession. We agree that we'll start talking once or twice a week and take it from there, and that he won't charge me.

I walk out of there not just floating on air, but hovering six feet above the ground. I pretty much remain that way, with only an occasional plummet, for the whole three years I'm involved with Ronnie before heading off to the high-mountain deserts of New Mexico.

MUSIC AND MAGIC

Ronnie started me off with a tailor-made reading list
as a way of introducing me to an informal study of
comparative religions. It included *The Function of the
Orgasm* by Wilhelm Reich; *Hara* by Karlfried Graf
Dürckheim; *Book of the It* by Georg Groddeck; *Tales
of Power* and *Journey to Ixtlan* by Carlos Castaneda;
Patañjali's *Yoga Sutras* (Ronnie once spent six months in
a cave in Sri Lanka, in silence, writing the sutras out by
hand); *Grist for the Mill* by Ram Dass; *Isis Unveiled* by
H. P. Blavatsky; *The Tibetan Book of the Dead* by Karma-
glin-pa; and *The Psychedelic Experience: A Manual
Based on the Tibetan Book of the Dead* by Timothy
Leary. He also said that everyone who's interested in
enlightenment should read the Bible from cover to cover
at least once in their lifetime (I still haven't and probably
never will, though). His list included all kinds of reading
matter ranging from Freud to Osho, enough to give me
a sufficiently broad overview and preponderance of
reference points to facilitate an optimal level of ongoing
dialogue between us.

The early sessions fell into a pattern: me talking
about myself, then him feeding back to me from oblique
angles – never for a moment pandering to my rational
mind's need to understand everything all at once, always
happy to leave me floundering in confusion. This would
be interspersed by me pressing him for a reaction.

Compulsively, I tried to draw him out emotionally, which usually took the form of me insulting him for being obscure and removed from everyday reality (and anything else I could think of at the time). He never once rose to the bait but evidently loved the sparring.

'Come on, get on the floor,' he said, smiling, as a response to one of my attacks. So I did and we had an arm-wrestling session. He won, partly because I was giggling so much at his unexpected competitiveness, and partly because he was – even acknowledging my occasionally overinflated opinion of myself – approximately 80,000 times more intelligent than I was and able to use it via his body.

'What was the point of that?' I asked.

Ronnie just looked at me and smiled with his left eyebrow rising a bit and said nothing. (It was a few years before I understood, and I'll tell you about that when we get to it.)

At the end of the session, he surprised and delighted me by inviting me that evening to a get-together of friends upstairs in his living quarters (his consulting room was on the ground floor).

'Ronnie invited me to come over tonight!' I squealed with excitement as I rushed into Johnny's flat afterwards. I always went there after a Ronnie session to relay what we'd talked about. Everyone talked to everyone about what Ronnie had said to them, pretty much all the time. When Ronnie said something to you, it was considered a gift, even if it was just to tell you to fuck off, which he was prone to do if he felt like it.

I arrived at Ronnie's house buzzing with a 20-year-old's nervous excitement tempered by self-consciousness. I sat in the corner watching in awe as all these groovy yoga teachers and therapists with shining eyes and great posture, confidence, and humour interacted with each other in an unusually sophisticated yet authentic way that I'd never previously witnessed in a group of people. Gradually, I got my bearings and settled into my skin.

When everyone was suitably warmed up, Ronnie sat down at the grand piano and started playing 'Bye Bye Blackbird.'

We'd spoken in sessions about music and how I played guitar and drums. 'Play the guitar,' he said, looking over at me.

I blushed. 'I can't really play to this. I don't know how to play these kinds of chords,' I replied, not having fully mastered the fretboard by then to play what I'd now call 'antique' songs.

'Play the bongos then.'

Fuck me, I thought to myself. *Play bongos to 'Bye Bye Blackbird'? What next?!* I was happy none of my friends could see me. Playing bongos to corny old tunes would have swung me so far off the cool scale that I would have been veritably ostracised for it.

Not that taking part in something so bizarre mattered to me. On the contrary, I found the implausibility extra charming. I was entranced by anything Ronnie did – it didn't matter what. As it happens, he was a fine pianist. I didn't know the words to the songs being sung, but I sat on the edge of the piano bench to Ronnie's right, so proud of myself as I tapped in accompaniment. As any percussionist will tell you, making those sing-along songs swing with bongos and piano is no mean feat. And I didn't accomplish it, but that didn't matter. It was such fun being in the place of honour, watching everyone singing and having such a great time, that I was melting in the joyfulness of it all.

I've been to many a spiritual event – in temples, monasteries, churches and what have you – yet never have I witnessed the presence of Spirit like I did at those singsongs. Conversations about it would ensue for days after. I was living in Little Venice at the time, when it was still hippie territory. Pretty much everyone except Ronnie lived around the same communal garden. If I had a yen for scriptwriting, the comings and goings-on around there would make for a stellar soap opera or sitcom.

Underlying all this was a drive to score recognition and acceptance from Ronnie. Everyone was at it. It's the guru syndrome, and it's unavoidable whenever a group habitually gathers around someone of extreme charisma and enlightenment. What was beautiful about this grouping was that you didn't have to go and live in some smelly old ashram. You could go through an equally life-transforming process right there in the heart of one of the nicest parts of London and have loads of fun while you were at it.

However, if I ever tried building on the bond I achieved with Ronnie the previous time I had seen him, whether it had been hanging out upstairs talking or playing music, or sitting in a session, it was in vain. While there was a continuity of dialogue at the soul level, there was none on the social level. I had to begin again every time. Everyone did. It wasn't just me.

At the time I was obsessed with Carlos Castaneda's Yaqui Indian sorcerer, don Juan. In general I was fascinated by people who knew how to perform real magic, Ronnie being one of them.

'I'm bored of sitting here talking all this crap. Go on, why don't you show me your power?' I goaded him from across the room one day.

'How do you think that would benefit you?' he asked.

But before I had time to answer, his face was as big as the sun and was *everywhere,* so all that existed was his face – directly in front of me. He held me like that (in what I later found out was a state almost the same as if you'd taken a powerful hallucinogen) and just as suddenly as it came about, his face receded until it was just him sitting in his armchair across the room, smiling at me with his left eyebrow raised in full extension.

'Fuck, wow, fuck, wow!' was all I could manage for a while. Then I blurted out, 'You've got to teach me that!'

'You already know how,' was all he said.

I do?! I thought to myself, *What the fuck is he talking about?* It was a question often on my lips in those days.

BORN AGAIN

Ronnie started holding Friday-night sessions at the church hall opposite his home. He'd invite people who were living in the houses he ran – people who'd be considered patients in the conventional mental-health framework – and a group of young therapists, yoga teachers, and me. There were about 50 people in all.

These sessions were composed of a series of trust games, such as falling backward and trusting that your partner would catch you; or two people face-to-face, holding hands, and spinning each other around, looking deep into each other's eyes to allay dizziness. The evening would culminate in a rebirthing session. A 'womb' would be created from eight people in a rugby scrum formation, and the one being reborn would be at the bottom of it, in fetal position. The scrum would act like a womb contracting. This would go on until the subject either made for a gap between the bodies with enough primal determination to be rescued by a 'midwife' or had to be delivered by "C-section".

Either way, a 20-minute interlude of pure baby-like consciousness would ensue, the subject being held in someone's arms like a newborn. The point of it was to take you all the way back to before the formation of the patterns of thought and behaviour that cripple your freedom of expression and so, if you were lucky, facilitate a fresh slate.

The rebirthing notion was something that Ronnie had developed in New York some years previously with a colleague. It had happened spontaneously when Ronnie observed that a young man she was treating looked as if he had never really been born fully into his body. So they set about re-creating the birth experience for him so that he could finally be born into himself. It worked, although it was evidently a risky business.

These sessions had an air of danger and excitement about them, imbued with the thrill of being included in the risky experiments of a living master and poet. Ronnie was a poet. He spoke in poetry. His voice was lyrical. He'd pace around the room as we were playing the trust games and seem to draw lines out of the air, which he'd deliver in his mesmerising Scottish tones. It was always an effort not to become totally entranced and forget what you were doing.

I suspect that this was what happened to the guy who was supposed to catch me in the 'free-fall' exercise the first time I went. Being naturally egalitarian, I went straight for one of the patients from the houses as my catcher, and in absolute (naïve) trust, I let myself fall backward, only to find him not there and me lying flat on my back on the floor with a sore head. From then on,

I'd only let myself be caught by my yoga-teacher friends, because they weren't nuts and were strong and reliable.

I remember discussing this trust issue with Ronnie. He could have gone into the whole notion of me creating it, giving the other the signal to let me down to justify an unconscious belief in others being unreliable. Or he could have gone into how the more I trust, the more the universe will look after me. But all he did was mumble, 'Ah, yes, of course . . . trust in Allah, but tie your camel first.' And he'd smile, as if to reaffirm that it's a paradox, and one that doesn't get resolved by discussing it.

Because it took eight or so people to form the human womb required for the rebirthing process (for which all the preceding trust games provided the preparation), and each womb required its own circle of onlookers, only two or three wombs could be formed at one time. Consequently, most people didn't get a chance to experience the rebirthing directly. This implied a willingness to derive satisfaction just from watching or co-facilitating a profound experience for someone else, which required a certain degree of generosity.

Ronnie never suggested that anyone be generous. He simply exuded the essence of selflessness, and it influenced those around him to be so, too. This extended to affording equal respect and attention to everyone present, no matter that in a different context they would be labelled as 'patient' or 'therapist'.

As far as Ronnie was concerned, we all came from the ineffable mystery and were thus essentially divine beings. And as essentially divine beings, everyone was due equal respect – respect for the divine. This didn't preclude being aware of and factoring in whatever apparent distortions might be present in whomever one was addressing at the time. We operated on at least two levels simultaneously.

Ronnie's art was being cognisant of all levels of mind and bringing them into the full glare of active consciousness, then being willing and progressively more able to accommodate the inevitable inherent paradox, rather than attempting to resolve it intellectually – to bear witness to, rather than trying to fix it. And this applied to both self and others. However, you wouldn't be able to bear witness to the other's existential state without trying to intervene in your bid to tidy up the world, unless you were first able to bear witness to your own existential state without trying to intervene. Maturity lay in being able to sit with the state, rather than trying to change it, knowing that as soon as you had integrated it and made it fully yours, it would change itself spontaneously.

Hence the need for the therapy sessions: to have Ronnie's help in facilitating the optimal mode in which to bear witness to the internal state. He'd talk about this, but only in response to my bringing it up by way of confirmation that I was getting it. Otherwise, this experience, and all the other profound aspects of his model, were conveyed simply in his way of being. He shone with the qualities he was imparting. He taught by example.

And a truly bold example it was.

Ronnie wasn't interested in playing it safe. Middle-class values weren't his concern. He was interested merely in truth and authenticity, in what was true for each person, and for each person to express that truth authentically.

I underwent the rebirthing process twice myself: the first time because I wanted and needed it; the second time was because it felt so utterly, indescribably, mind-shatteringly wonderful the first time that I just wanted to do it again, being greedy for the intensity of the experience. I've had many intense experiences in my life, being of that propensity, and rebirthing Ronnie-style is right up there at the top of the heap.

The first time it started off all cosy. I sat on my heels, bent forward at the hips in the fetal-like yogic child posture, with all these kind, warm people lying on top of and all around me. One of them was holding my head down to my chest to lengthen my spine, making me feel perfectly loved, safe, and protected from the world . . . just as it would have been at various phases in the actual uterus. But after a while, the pressure became uncomfortable, and I started trying to move. In response to my movement, the 'womb' contracted and tightened up all around and on top of me, making me even more uncomfortable, until I went totally primal, using every ounce of strength in my body, roaring with the urge to break free. The womb tightened even more. My strength went. I flopped. Then the primal urge took me again. Roaring and pushing with all my might, I managed to move the womb, but it just tightened up on me again. Finally, this intensely claustrophobic, impotent sensation became too much to bear, and I opened my eyes. I realised they'd been shut the whole time. With my eyes open, I spotted a slight gap between two people and made for it with absolute determination, like a missile being fired. The next thing I knew, someone was pulling me out (there was a designated 'midwife' for each 'womb'), and then I was held, cradled like a baby in someone's arms. As it happens, they were the arms of my (female) friend Jeb Walker, whom I'll tell you about later, as she was and remains one of my greatest teachers, but it could have been anyone who'd be willing to be present enough to hold me and bear witness to my experience without interfering.

I lay there like that with my head in her lap for 20 minutes. My mind was completely empty, making no associations whatsoever, just like newborns who know nothing of the world and can make no associations, other than the feeling of love and nurturing coming from the ones holding them.

Naturally, the after-effects of the experience were profound and lasted a few weeks as the memories flooded back from even before my birth – all the way back to conception. I was actually able to vividly recall my father's sperm implanting at one point – make of that what you will.

The effect this had on those who'd been experiencing what even now is conventionally described as schizophrenia was equally profound. I saw people previously semi-catatonic rise up from those sessions smiling and talking as if they'd had their slates wiped clean and had just returned from a remarkable voyage somewhere in the netherworlds. It was nothing short of miraculous, yet the method wasn't mysterious but totally mechanical, logical and obvious.

The process was also rich in metaphor. I often marvel, for instance, how all I had to do was open my eyes and I was then free to escape constriction.

But the whole thing was so underplayed.

Everyone knew that Ronnie was a miracle worker. Everyone was learning from him, each in their own way, how to work miracles themselves. And nothing needed to be said about it. Imagine how that would be sold these days in the marketplace of the self-development world.

But the rebirthing sessions couldn't happen now because the insurance premiums would be too high. People didn't have a litigious consciousness in those days, and the disease of greed hadn't set in just yet. Margaret Thatcher hadn't taken power; and her ethos of greed – which was spawned in the USA, championed by her in the UK, and subsequently spread worldwide to produce this current multilevel survival crisis of ours – had not quite taken hold of the world's psyche.

This meant that mavericks like Ronnie could work and express themselves freely. Yes, it was risky; anything could happen. This was real life, with no safety nets. That way of working could never have continued because the methods initiated by the greats back then became mass-market fare, and the litigiousness and greed grew exponentially. I suspect that's because the intelligence guiding the collective mind knows that this level of experience isn't necessary anymore. It was something required at the time, in a similar way to the radical influence of LSD on the culture, but which is no longer appropriate.

This on-the-edge reality was appropriate then – certainly for me. It was precisely what I'd wanted when I first imagined studying 'wisdom' from Ronnie. What is wisdom good for, if not for dealing with other people in a way that promotes healing in the broader sense? And what could be a more potent metaphor for that than using this absurdly powerful technique for wiping the slate clean of accumulated psycho-emotional pain?

Naturally, I say all this in retrospect. At the time, I was too engrossed in the experience to know that at some point, the world would be different. I never imagined in a million years that the business of self-development would reach such mainstream proportions, and thereby be necessarily watered down to marketable and relatively anodyne chunks.

This was pioneer stuff, on the forefront of the human-consciousness experiment. We may have been in a church hall in a London suburb with a man from Glasgow talking mellifluously as we engaged in the extreme sport of psychodynamic slate-cleaning, but we could just as easily have been in the high Himalayas with an Indian master of the ancient yogic arts. There was an archetypal quality about Ronnie and the events he facilitated. All present were transported to the realm of hyperspace, hyperreality, where true transformation occurs. But we weren't interested in manifesting things. We weren't looking at how any of this could be to our material gain. This was innocent, free of marketing or the drive to market. This was pure. Ronnie was pure.

He used to drink and smoke, and goodness knows what else. We all did in those days, but this had nothing to do with purity levels. The purity was in the authenticity and lack of pretension – rare qualities then and now – so thanks be to the ineffable presence for expressing itself through Ronnie for the time it did. Our world is vastly richer for it.

One day about 40 of us went off on a bus to Shepperton Studios, west of London, to take part in a film to demonstrate the work done in the Friday-night sessions. I'd learned the words to some of the sing-along songs by then, so on the way back I was singing merrily with everyone else. (I had no bongos to hide behind anyway.) It's funny how I remember the event first from

the back end of it, because the filming itself that led up
to the bus ride home was, and remains, one of the more
extraordinary events of my life.

The set was huge with all white floors and walls:
it was like being in heaven. All of us 'angels' were
wearing brightly coloured yoga-style outfits, which were
fashionable at the time. I remember the opening scene was
all of us spread out at random spots in the room, standing
perfectly still like human statues – disconnected, no one
looking at anyone else. It was meant to represent the
disassociated, alienated state. Ronnie strode between us
talking. He walked slowly around, plucking his impromptu
poetry out of the studio air. The filming progressed through
the trust games on to the rebirthing process itself, during
which I had a notable-for-me, mind-over-matter lesson.

Jeb Walker was the rebirthing subject. A real flaming-
haired beauty, the impact of the vividness of her physical
presence against the white was startling. We, in the
surrounding circle, had to sit around the 'womb' without
moving for well over an hour. I had chosen to sit on my
heels. The floor was concrete and unforgiving.

After ten minutes or so, I started getting pins and
needles, but had I moved, it would have delayed things
by causing them to start shooting the scene again. I had
no choice but to use my mind to overcome the pain, and
within seconds, it had vanished. It stayed away for the
duration. Although not as dramatic as mind-over-matter
examples go, my ability to do that provided a benchmark

for endurance of all kinds that still works for me to this day. So does the blessed memory of standing up afterwards and feeling the joyous release in my knees.

And then came the bus ride back with me joining in at last, overcoming my shyness to sing old songs, totally letting go and abandoning myself, acting out some sort of corny movie script all the way home.

Ronnie was beautiful that day: like God walking around, working the room. The added element of being filmed – so commonplace today with the whole reality-TV phenomenon, but rare back then – did nothing to reduce the authenticity of everyone present, especially Ronnie. On the contrary, it somehow seemed to add to the experience as if we were all contributing something momentous to the greater human experiment.

Ronnie was well ahead of the game in terms of fusing the depths of self-development with various forms of media – not just film, but also spoken word and music. His album, *Life before Death,* for instance, was a work of sheer genius. It was produced by Stephen Lipson at a studio in St Johns Wood in London. The studio was on haunted premises that used to be a church and crypt. Strangely and coincidentally, it was first bought by the guy who managed my early music career, and then by Yehudi Gordon, as the centre for his obstetrics practice (but more about him later).

Ronnie's piano-playing on the album and the additional musical accompaniment was sublime, the poetry profound, the vocal delivery supreme, the effect on the listener radical, and the fusion of spoken-word poetry over music seminal and completely original.

In those days, the marketplace had no openings for anything outside of the given box. Even today, with all the access afforded to innovators by the Internet, it's still relatively tricky to introduce left-field offerings. However, back then there really were no outlets for truly edgy content, whether in film or music, unless it fell into a specific genre that already existed. (Creating new genres is something that no one should undertake lightly. To that I can attest from experience.) For Ronnie, the challenge was exponentially harder, and I admired his courage in doing so. I vowed to carry that experiment on in my own style on his behalf when he died.

The problem with attempting to create new styles by fusing your own various talents is that the world gets used to you being one thing and finds it hard to see you as something else. It's as if you're only entitled to be respected or taken seriously for one aspect of your creative expression – as though it wouldn't be fair otherwise.

I mention this to demonstrate yet again how the requisite influences for the various creative avenues and work templates I would develop as time went on were all so elegantly introduced into my life as if according to some meticulously devised plan – like the pattern of lines on the palm or the configuration of stars in one's astrological chart. And always mixed in was the recurring theme of the realm of sound with psycho-spiritual exploration.

*** ***

'Have you ever fantasised having sex with your mother?' Ronnie asked me this one day, out of the blue, in all seriousness, one eyebrow raised in curious anticipation of my response.

'No, I haven't,' I replied with a squirm. 'Why do you ask that?'

'It's a powerful technique.'

'For what? Making yourself vomit?'

'For getting to understand that your mother is a woman and you're a man. For understanding there's another aspect to your relationship with her and with the world-as-mother.'

I did get around to doing that spontaneously 16 years later, not in a sexually arousing way, but as a visualisation, and it did yield a powerful healing effect. In fact, it was directly after my experiment that my mother and I, always at odds over one thing or another, spontaneously became friends at a deep level and have remained so since.

I mention this simply to convey the way Ronnie had of being able to shock you into an altered state. But if I had to condense everything I learned from hanging out with him to a single kernel of wisdom, it would be that everything in the universe consists essentially of consciousness; and that consciousness controls your state of health, the state of harmony in your relationships with others, and your levels of success in your dealings with others. Everything is mind, in other words. Also, when you're living from a state of pure compassion, you compel the universe to treat you with compassion.

That compassion derives from remembering that you were once a fetus and so was everyone else, in utero and dependent upon the mysterious maternal force – the Tao, if you like – causing the placenta to conduct life to you. Ultimately, what goes on in your life on the local plane from day to day is relatively inconsequential compared to what goes on in the eternal moment, access to which is gained through spiritual practice. By engaging in diligent daily practice of your spiritual techniques, whatever they are, you acquire the ability to cause everyday reality to morph for the better by intention alone. Moreover, this ability naturally extends to being able to correct malfunctions of the mind, body, spirit, or material circumstances for others as well as yourself.

I remember once in Little Venice, overlooking that vast communal garden, I stayed up all night on acid, doing yoga and tai chi and handwriting a whole book to Ronnie about my thoughts, observations, and feelings. It was good, too – my first ever book. I gave it to him the next time I saw him. 'I've written you a short book about everything in my mind.'

He took a quick glance and handed it back to me with one of his enigmatic questions, one that has fuelled an ongoing internal debate and investigation about it to this day. 'How do you know it's *your* mind?' That was all he said. But when he died, I inherited the pen he wrote many of his books with, perhaps as a message to write him an update.

Another time, I told Ronnie that he was a wimp because he wasn't into martial arts, so he started wrestling with me. It ended with both of us on the floor with him tickling me. I'm very ticklish and was soon up and out of his grasp declaring a truce – and he was laughing hysterically.

One day I showed up for a session with Ronnie, complaining about how filthy London was, how diminished life was in the urban sprawl, how the whole thing was a waste of time that only lands you in the graveyard . . . and for fuck's sake, what's the point of it all? Then I spontaneously launched into: 'Let's go to Mexico and build an R. D. Laing Centre! I'll get the financing. I'll set it up and we'll all go, and you can do your thing over there.'

It was a wild and ebullient outpouring – one I hadn't thought through. The notion hadn't even crossed my mind until it came out of my mouth. The proposed location was based solely on my fascination with Carlos Castaneda's

Yaqui Indian sorcerer who had ostensibly lived in the
Mexican Sonoran Desert across the border from Arizona.
As soon as I'd blurted it out, I felt stupid.

'Okay.'

'What?'

'Okay. Organise it.'

'Really?'

'Yes. And as for the filth of the city, a rose is still a rose
. . . even if it's a bit dirty.'

So suddenly there I was with a project: a reason, a
focus, something practical and huge. It would require
persuading approximately 20 families to pick up and
move to the wilderness of northern Mexico, although I
knew this would be easier to do with Ronnie on board.
I think everyone would have followed him anywhere at
that point. But I also had to find willing investors to back
something that wasn't an easy sell.

I imagined people would come in droves from the
United States, as Ronnie was extremely popular in
America back then, having been a college-campus
counterculture hero with his book *The Politics of
Experience*. I envisioned myself running the place, as
I was good at logistics and organisation and enjoyed
working with people. I could see myself carrying on my
learning of 'wisdom' by just being around Ronnie. The
fantasy of hanging out with all these spectacular people
appealed to me in the same fantastic way as, say, the
images of a group of superheroes sequestered safely

from the world conjured up by reading Ayn Rand's *Atlas Shrugged*. In reality, though, it probably would have imploded and turned out more like *Lord of the Flies*.

It soon became clear that the whole idea was really a device I was unconsciously using to be accepted as more of a senior tribe member. The practicalities involved were simply too unwieldy to make the plan actually doable.

In addition, everyone had their little kids at school and were all living comfortably in nice flats in the then post-hippie paradise of London's Little Venice. It wouldn't be easy to convince the group that this madcap scheme made good sense. Although, as I said, they might have been persuaded had Ronnie said that he was really heading off there. And Ronnie, although the most existentially experimental man I'd ever met, was also a leading, if highly controversial, figure in his field with a big life going on in London. He wasn't going to just hop on a plane and vanish into the Mexican desert without a lot of things being very well sorted out in advance. Likewise, people willing to invest in that sphere back then were more interested in what were called 'health farms' – the equivalent of today's spas. As I began to make my rounds of the money people, I soon discovered that the idea of a centre to explore the uncharted regions of the human psyche using maverick techniques didn't have instant investor appeal.

But then came the maudlin apocalyptic strains of Pink Floyd's *The Wall,* along with Margaret Thatcher's Protect and Survive project. The former set the end-of-the-world tone. The latter was a leaflet advising citizens how to avoid death in the case of a USSR nuclear attack on the UK. This mostly involved advice on how to hole yourself up in the smallest room in the house with supplies of canned food and fluids, and to stuff clothes in the cracks under the doors to keep out the radiation. I found this rather comical and destabilising. It added to the generally depressing mood of the country and made me start thinking about heading off somewhere more amenable to happy living.

One day while I was walking slowly around Watkins bookshop off Charing Cross Road (which at the time was one of the only places in London where you could buy books related to self-development and metaphysics), a book literally jumped off the shelf at me as if it had springs beneath it. It was the *Book of the Hopi* by Frank Waters. In it, Waters translated the ancient prophecy that the world would reach an untenable level of insanity and then self-destruct via atomic warfare, and that the place to be was the Hopi homelands in northern Arizona. It wasn't so much that scenario as the descriptions of the kachina dolls and the dancing that got to me, and I determined at once that I'd head off that way. I also started getting the sensation – psychotic or channelled, who can ever tell? – that I was being psychically drawn to the Native Americans.

I saw it all in a flash: I was to live with the Indians. And there wasn't time to waste.

My father thought that I'd totally lost my marbles – like I'd watched too many *Lone Ranger* episodes as a kid. I then went to see Ronnie. 'I haven't got time to hang about and do this project. I'm heading off now . . . join me if you want.'

This was me saying that I was going it alone, breaking away from the king and his tribe after investing so much energy into him and it, in order to find my own path. It was momentous.

'I'll ask the others and see what they say, but I can't imagine many thinking it would be wise just now,' he answered with utmost compassion.

*** ***

When I returned from New Mexico four years later, I was staying at Jeb Walker's home, and one night she threw me a welcome-back party. That was the next time I saw Ronnie. He walked in and we hugged. Then he sat down on some cushions, and I sat in front of him – the disciple returned from his vision quest, dressed all in white as I was wont to do in those days, perhaps unconsciously promoting the notion of New Mexican purity in filthy London.

'I issue you a challenge!' he said.

'What kind of challenge?'

He didn't answer.

'Indian arm wrestling?'

Nothing.

'Full-on wrestling?'

Still nothing.

'Oh, come on, Ronnie!' My curiosity was now piqued, and I was delighted to be back in the game with him again. He didn't mention it again.

A little later with about 30 people – all therapists or yoga teachers – sitting on the cushions lining three walls of the immensely long room, he started pacing up and down the length of the space, looking at no one in particular. But all eyes were on him, as usual.

He started talking about Jacqueline du Pré, the master cellist stricken by severe multiple sclerosis, whom he was treating at the time. Everyone fell silent. The story was so tragic that he was crying as he was telling it. He wasn't wiping the tears away or trying to hide them. He'd glance at me as if to let me know that he was showing me how it was done. (At the time, I didn't relate this to my initial confession to him all those years before about not being able to cry.) He kept on crying as he spoke, and the snot was streaming from his nose onto his cardigan sweater. He did nothing to wipe it away. He was fully immersed in the moment. (Total immersion was key to everything he taught.) Soon every single person was moved to tears. Then he suddenly stopped, cracked a wry gag, and the party atmosphere started back up again.

A couple of weeks later, there was another party. At one point I was standing in the kitchen playing the guitar and had a rapt audience of about 13 crammed in listening. I was on form and playing well. All of a sudden, Ronnie popped his head around the door, and instantly everyone's attention went to him. I carried on playing and smiled at him.

'You can't play the fucking guitar!' he goaded in his best Scottish street accent.

I stopped playing. 'What do you mean? Yes I can!' Then I realised I'd been had. That was the challenge, and he'd beaten me. He'd thrown me off my power, off my centre, and had done it extremely neatly by referring back to the time I took up the position of chief bongo player at the sing-alongs. He had a way of tying things up nice and tidy like that.

I laughed and started playing again until I'd retrieved the crowd, then got bored with it and went into the other room, where Ronnie was sitting holding court.

'Nice one. You got me, but why must we have this antagonistic thing going on between us, do you think? Can't we stop it now?'

He laughed. 'Okay.'

Okay. That was the last thing Ronnie ever said to me, which I guess is a good last thing to say to someone.

Shortly after, he went off to live in the mountains of Austria.

A few years passed with no contact. Then in 1989 (the year of the birth of The Barefoot Doctor), he was due to come to London in September, and we were to meet up. I remember one day toward the end of August, feeling so excited to be seeing him again. I almost couldn't believe that it was actually going to happen. And I was right.

Ronnie died on 23rd August, 1989, the day of Jeb's birthday, playing tennis in Saint-Tropez, and winning.

His last words, when told the doctor was coming as he lay dying from a heart attack, were: 'What fucking doctor!' It was if to say there wasn't a doctor on the planet who could touch his level, and if he couldn't fix it, no doctor could.

And he was right. But sometimes I muse that he was talking about The Barefoot Doctor – that's which fucking doctor! It makes me laugh. But I wasn't laughing then. I got straight in the car and drove five hours to Jeb's farm in Wales; it seemed the only place to be. And I cried and I cried and I cried – for three whole days I cried. Ronnie's medicine worked. I've never had a problem crying since.

During those three days, I felt as if I were receiving transmissions from him, as if he were passing on his inheritance to me. A few people said they experienced something similar during that time, each in their own way. It wasn't necessarily all formulated and packaged, just as it wasn't in real life. But it all came through clear as daylight nonetheless; and the gist of it was to be present, be compassionate, give your all, and don't let the bastards grind you down. That had been one of Ronnie's frequent sayings: 'It's a fine life as long as you don't let the bastards grind you down.' It still gives me succour to this day.

Whether or not it's proper to mention this, as it's entirely subjective, I'm going to say it anyway: since he died, he nudges me every now and then. It's always at crucial moments, often when I'm in a crisis or am helping someone who is. I hear his voice coming through loud and clear, far louder and clearer than had I been imagining it, and he'll tell me just what I need to do to help or resolve the situation.

Ronnie made it safe to explore the realms of my own psyche that I would have never dared to look at otherwise. He made it safe for people to be themselves, however mad that self might be at the time. He made it safe to acknowledge that we're living in a global mental asylum. He made it safe to question the veracity of the world's common sense. He made it safe to stop playing the silly games of society and be real.

Recently, I was listening to a recording of Ronnie being interviewed, shortly before he died, by Anthony Clare, a psychiatrist who had programmes on the BBC. I was amazed to discover that Ronnie had considered himself to be depressed. I'd never even considered that possibility, so powerful a presence was he. Yet I finally understood that holding the world's suffering as he did – without distracting himself from it or sanitising it away – must have been profoundly distressing. I was shocked for having been so self-centred never to have considered how life must have been from his perspective – like Beethoven not being able to aurally appreciate the wonder of his own music.

But maybe most importantly, Ronnie reinforced my understanding that life begins at conception and our subsequently unfolding relationship with the world is predicated entirely on our experience growing in the womb, our passage through the birth canal, and those earliest days out on the planet after birth. If all that is managed properly, we have a chance to grow fully into ourselves. To the extent that this process is distorted, as it invariably is, we split off crucial aspects of ourselves, both individually and collectively, thus co-creating the hugely split-off, distorted, global society we now live in.

So let's say someone – me, for instance – had an interest in contributing something of real value to the collective. I would have to view everyone in the entire world as newborn babies and speak to them on that level in order to heal, or make whole, the rifts both within and without.

Ronnie taught me to respect babies as divine, all-knowing beings, fresh out of the heavenly realms, rather than diminished humans. This helped inspire me to focus much of my work on healing these little ones for a long phase during the 1980s, which I'll tell you about a bit later.

*** ***

Chapter Seven

Living the Tao

When I initially tried to understand what it meant to follow the Tao, I was fully aware that Taoism was a metaphor rather than a religion. You didn't have to officially *be* a Taoist, wear a funny hat, or walk around with a beatific expression on your face quoting Lao-tzu in order to be in the flow. And there are many people who live according to Taoist precepts and follow Tao-like masters without ever having heard of Taoism. After all, this philosophy is merely one way of describing the keys that can open you up to a certain transcendent state of mind and being, which leads to a particular way of going about things in the world and having your needs provided for without striving or straining.

JEB WALKER

Jeb wouldn't have described herself as a Taoist. She wouldn't have said she was following the Tao, living her life according to *wu-wei* (the notion that you can manifest what you want simply by seeing it so in your mind, then letting go and allowing it to happen). But of all the people I've ever met, she embodied – and still embodies – the principles. Her life remains living proof that *wu-wei* works.

When I met Jeb in the mid-1970s, she was a flaming-haired, yoga-practising beauty of 30, married to Peter – the yoga teacher I told you about earlier, who went on to become the world's leading proponent of baby massage.

I fell in love, in the unconditional, universal sense, with both of them simultaneously and would spend hours at their place talking about the deepest aspects of being human. I'd always been given to extremely honest communication, and had found most people unable to meet me on that level without the obfuscations of pride and falsehood getting in the way. Whenever I encountered folks who were willing and able to be real, I'd relish and celebrate it, and still do. After all, it's a rare phenomenon in this world where pretension, lies, and hypocrisy are the more general currency. When I met Jeb, I saw absolute truth in her eyes. No airs or graces, she was beautiful without vanity, wise without arrogance, humble without self-deprecation, kind without indulgence, honest without brutality, and gracious without self-consciousness. Having grown up on Old Kent Road in South London (then and now a rough part of town), she was no stranger to the toughness of life, no stranger to the ways of the world's con artists. Yet she never lost her faith in the innate goodness of humanity, and although she has always worried about the world and the stupidity of the species, she still maintains that faith to this day.

At the time, she was supplementing her living as an artist by looking after Ronnie's children: Adam, who, sadly, died in tragic circumstances not long ago; Natasha; and Max. But she did this as a friend rather than an employee. She perhaps understood Ronnie better than anyone. I used to spend hours talking to her about my relationship and dialogue with him, and I'm sure that I wouldn't have derived the value I did from it were it not for her help at every turn. So when I talk about my training with Ronnie, I'd only be describing half the story if I didn't mention Jeb.

Jeb has never had ambition, other than to see everyone around her happy. For her, 'everyone around her' includes the entirety of humanity. She doesn't have to train herself to meditate for the good of the world. She doesn't have to force herself to be kind or selfless in her prayers. She is naturally so. She has never attempted to achieve status or importance. She has merely lived her life in kindness and authenticity. As a result, more than anyone I know, she is now probably better set up to withstand potentially pernicious effects as the world (as we know it) rapidly approaches meltdown.

She and her current partner, Mike, a don of dons, live on a fully self-sufficient farm in the wilds of West Wales. They produce their own hydroelectricity and food, and have their own freshwater well. They also have the space to house all of their loved ones if necessary. I personally know no one who has it more together, and none of it was contrived or engineered. It all happened for her by *wu-wei*. And even with all that, she is by no means rustic and counts more than a few celebrities among her closest friends – not that she's bothered by that kind of nonsense.

Nor was she bothered about Ronnie's fame back then in the mid-1970s. She just loved him for the amazing man he was.

The first time I sat with Jeb, we looked into each other's eyes for quite a while.

'Wow, you're really sad in there, aren't you,' she said with utmost compassion, understanding and empathy.

No one had ever spotted that aspect of myself before. I'd always been aware of it, buried under the surface: sadness about the cruel games people play; about the meanness with which people treat each other; about the pain of inevitable separation from those you love; about the shock of being on the planet, no longer safe in the womb; about the hard-hearted greed, vanity, and deceit of the world at large; and that generalised indefinable beautiful/terrible anguish in the soul that is paradoxically a joy to feel, so poignant is it.

That was Jeb's gift to me and to the world: authenticity, understanding and acceptance. That and the encouragement to keep faith in the old ways of honour, decency, reciprocity, kindness and tolerance, come what may.

Once, before Ronnie died, I was experiencing a personal crisis. I was going through that classic early-30s passage of coming to terms with various disparate elements of self, and found myself drawn to the farm to talk it through with Jeb. After she listened to everything I had to say, sitting there at the old stone hearth, she said in all seriousness, 'Steve, you should probably go outside and have a nervous breakdown. It'd be the best thing for you.'

So I did. I went outside and wandered the mountainside, with the wind blowing off the Irish Sea chilling my bones, and I completely let go of my rational mind. At one point, I found myself sitting on a rock in the rain, talking out loud: my higher self speaking to my local self. 'You'd best get up and go inside now. You can't just sit here on this rock in the rain – you'll freeze to death.'

As I stood up, my whole worldview suddenly cleared. My heart was instantly light and happy, as if someone had cast a benign spell on me, and I was practically skipping back to the house. Jeb was sitting by the fire. She smiled and winked as if she knew exactly what had happened, as if she'd been with me the whole time and accepted that the crisis was over.

She'd facilitated a major turning point for me and provided me with the proof of this truth: *When things look their bleakest, if you surrender and let your higher self take over, you'll be delivered back to safety no matter what.*

GREGORY BATESON: AN UNNECESSARY DISUNITY

Gregory Bateson was an anthropologist, biologist, mathematician, philosopher, master of metaphysics, and mentor to Ronnie. At a meeting I once had with him, I'd just struggled through one of his books, *Mind and Nature: A Necessary Unity.* It succinctly sets down the laws of existence in about as profound and profoundly head-crunching a way as you'll ever find. While he spoke about the state of unnecessary disunity with the self, my input to the conversation consisted of, and was limited to, the odd self-conscious 'Hmm' or 'Wow'. He was so intellectually advanced that I hardly understood a word he was saying, but it didn't matter. I understood him on a heart level even if my intellect was comparatively in shreds.

Perceiving my limited capacity, Gregory generously told me one thing in summary to help me out, and it radically altered my entire relationship with ontological reality from then on. That's why I've included it here.

'There's no such thing as objective reality,' he stated. 'As far as we're concerned here,' referring to our conversation and to existence in general, 'we can only experience reality subjectively.' From this I inferred that reality can only really be subjective as far as each of us is concerned on the everyday local level. In other words, there's no absolute truth . . . at least not one that we – in our stepped-down, localised, human form – can appreciate intellectually. We give life all the meaning it has for us.

FRITJOF CAPRA

You can spend years with some teachers to learn one thing, yet with others it takes just a single moment to learn a thousand things. I only met Ronnie's friend, quantum physicist Fritjof Capra, once, for a few minutes. Yet the impact he made on me profoundly shaped my direction from then on. I'd read and relished his book *The Tao of Physics,* which for the first time ever showed how the leading minds on the exploratory cutting edge of existence had come around to saying the same thing about the existential underpinning of reality as the ancient Taoist sages – just in different words.

I personally needed no proof of that. As far as I was and am concerned, demanding hard evidence when you can experience it for yourself with your own senses is just for babies. And I daresay that those who come up with the proof are of the same mind. Otherwise, how could they think laterally enough to intuit the answers? They'd be too constricted by convention.

It was clearly evident that Fritjof wasn't coming from the need to prove anything; it was more to simply share his youthful exhilaration at discovering such a strong thread of continuity and universality in a particular lineage of enlightened consciousness. He was coming from the position of humility, always irresistible in an out-and-out genius. He was in deference to higher wisdom that was proving itself in the completion of this circle between the ancient and modern sages, and their investigations into the Tao and the quantum field, respectively.

I congratulated him on his book and his refined mind. Then I explained that my interest in his field (the Tao and the quantum field) arose from practising tai chi, which I considered to be the dance of ultimate wisdom. He put his palm on my upper arm and started moving me around, subtly forcing me to centre.

'Very good,' he said, as if he could tell that I had the entire universe figured out, then gave me one of the most encouraging smiles I've ever seen. It was enough to sustain me through subsequent periods of doubt on the path of enquiry to which I was dedicating my life. For this profound, though fleeting, service, Fritjof must have his place in this book.

FRANCIS HUXLEY

Having been in awe of Aldous Huxley since I was a boy, it was exciting to meet his nephew, Francis Huxley, a good friend of Ronnie's and a master explorer. He invited me over before I set off for New Mexico, in the manner of the old explorer don offering some parting advice to the whippersnapper fledgling explorer setting off on his first grand expedition.

Mass travel only began in earnest toward the end of the 1980s. Although we've grown accustomed to moving around the globe with relative ease, we have to remember that not long ago, there was little in the way of low-cost air travel or airports in every small city on the planet. There was no Internet or mobile phones, and as a result, much less information was freely available. This meant that everywhere was, or at least seemed, much further away and exotic. Intrepid travellers really had to be keen to find things out about where they wanted to go, especially if it was off the beaten track.

Francis was happy to help me find out what I could on my mission to live with the Native Americans. He showed me slides of New Mexico that thrilled my senses. And all through his commentary, he rolled his *R*s in a most pronounced theatrical fashion, with the effect that in every instance I'd sink deeper into a trance.

At one point, while showing me objects from obscure spots all around the world, he thrust a carved wooden penis into my hand that a witch doctor had given to him in Africa, and told me to rub the end of it, as if rubbing Aladdin's magic lamp. This, he said, would bring me great virility that would sustain me on the adventure ahead. It was an odd moment – his voice bristling with energy like a sorcerer from some *Lord of the Rings*-style Hollywood epic.

His gift, and the reason why I include him here, was to informally initiate me as an explorer, a model I've been working off ever since as I relate the various phases of the adventure.

*** ***

Chapter Eight
High-Country Deserts

So there I suddenly was one day, as if by magic, high up on the Colorado Plateau in the Hopi lands of Northern Arizona, having left my beautiful London life behind in search of deeper wisdom and adventure. In my quest for the edge, I was on the actual edge of a flat roof, which was on the edge of a precipitous cliff, overlooking what might easily have been an endless expanse of moonscape were it not for the occasional shrub poking out from a rock.

I was practising tai chi to ground and orient myself, and to figure out how I was ever going to find the keeper of the fabled Hopi prophecy. I'd naïvely imagined that it was going to be a simple matter: roll up at Hopi HQ and ask at the reception desk to meet with the prophecy keeper. But if you ever visit Hopi lands for yourself, you'll soon note that their residents are a far more discreet bunch than that. Finding anyone in particular from scratch would be more unlikely than finding a needle in a stack of haystacks.

I was feeling a bit bewildered, and whenever I'm out of sorts, I tend to do tai chi, as it has a surprisingly de-bewildering effect. So there I was, overlooking the edge of sanity (or so it felt), doing 'waving hands in the clouds', a repetitive blocking and striking-to-the-side manoeuvre that occurs three times in the long form. Out of the corner of my eye, each time I turned my body to the right, I spotted a turquoise convertible cruising up the winding high-desert road toward me from miles away, getting closer and closer.

I continued with the tai chi until a mop of golden hair poked up over the edge of the roof, swiftly followed by a guy named Jeff, or so I quickly learned as soon as I finished the form (I never interrupt my practice unless there's a life-threatening emergency).

Jeff was an art dealer who worked with the Hopi Indians and had just driven the 2,500 miles or so from New York. He was a tai chi practitioner himself and had been astounded to see someone practising it on a roof in Hopi land. Bear in mind that hardly anyone did (or had even heard of) tai chi back then, especially in this Arizona moonscape. So Jeff simply had to stop and introduce himself, and we fell into talking about our respective lives and discovered many parallels.

'Hey, I'm going to dinner at a friend's here tonight,' he said. 'Would you like to come? His name's Thomas Banyacya. He's the Keeper of the Prophecy.'

'Fuck me!' I blurted out. It was the most eloquent expression I could muster in my utter astonishment. 'Yes, please!'

THOMAS BANYACYA

That evening we drove together in Jeff's convertible, the moonscape already starting to look more amenable, more lovable – and me feeling the elation that comes with instances of extreme serendipity. We arrived at Thomas's house, a humble adobe structure, where we were invited in by his wife. Thomas walked in and immediately filled the room with his presence. He and Jeff greeted each other with a manly hug, then Jeff introduced me. We shook hands and smiled warmly and deeply into each other's eyes in silence for quite some time, gazing into each other's souls and hearts.

'Come, sit down.' He gestured for us to sit around the table.

The conversation soon turned to world affairs. The USSR had just invaded Afghanistan, and the West was threatening nuclear war; Pink Floyd had brought out

The Wall; Margaret Thatcher was heavily promoting the culture of selfishness; and Jimmy Carter, leader of the free world in such perilous times, seemed too nice a guy to be dealing with the spectre of a third world war. At least that was the take I put forward.

Thomas's perspective was somewhat different. The forces of darkness were fighting with the forces of light because the light was growing stronger, and we needed to be strong ourselves in order to support it. If we did so, we'd be all right.

'I get that in theory,' I offered. 'But I can't help feeling cynical when I think of all those warheads lined up on both sides. I can't help thinking that when boys have guns, they eventually tend to use them.' I was talking slowly, extending my vowel sounds, as I'd learned by then that the American ear wasn't used to the relatively more clipped staccato sounds of the English voice, and often people couldn't understand a word I said.

Still, Thomas was looking at me uncomprehendingly.

'Do you know what I mean?' I asked, like a teenager.

'Yes, I do know what you mean, but you've become too cynical. You've believed too much in the illusion of power and not enough in power itself.'

Jeff was sitting back peering at me: watching me visibly shape-shifting no doubt, as my mental model morphed in a bid to recalibrate itself against this unexpected influx of 'heavy' data. I knew Thomas was right. It was like sitting with Geshe at the meditation sessions, or with Ronnie when he was hypnotising me. The material plane is an illusion. It's generated by an unseen presence: God, the Tao, the Great Spirit. Only *that* is real; everything else is relative. If you want to change the merely relative, do so by changing your relationship with the real. This was the experience when sitting with such men of power. It was unspoken and incontrovertible.

'Yes, I see that,' I said. 'But how? How do we change it?'

'By praying. By "illusioning" it away.' He smiled warmly and provocatively in a playful way as he pronounced *illusioning,* as if to imply that this Americanisation, this modernisation of the concept of prayer, was his concession to Jeff and me and our culture.

'By praying, we can change everything.' He went on: 'Now you need to purify your mind of these cynical beliefs. You have to pray a lot – that will purify you. Then you can help others. There are many who will need it.' He stated it all sternly but kindly, then fell silent.

We three sat respectfully in that silence for a few minutes until his wife brought the food in. Then we started talking about the Hopi lands. Thomas explained how there was division there as well: the progressives wanted to allow uranium mining for the money; but the traditionalists felt, believed and knew that if it happened, it would destroy the integrity of the sacred land and their spiritual way, which is so *intimately* associated with the land. Also, it would actually herald the end of this world as we know it. That's why it was so important for us to pray now.

Then we prayed. It was the first time I'd ever been involved in Native American prayers and found it deeply sobering. It was completely natural. Thomas didn't adopt a false voice, as is the way with many Western religious intermediaries, like they're playing a role. Thomas *wasn't* playing a role. He was simply, humbly talking to the Creator as if he were talking to his own brother. He wasn't looking up to the ceiling, nor was he holding his hands together. His tone wasn't reverent, but it was respectful. No formality or show – just pure respect.

Thomas prayed for understanding and peace in the hearts of his brothers and sisters, for me, for Jeff, for his wife, for the Hopi nation, for all the tribes, for all people, for all nations. Then there was absolute silence: no car noise, no phones, no electricity hum, no speaking. Just the sound of the breeze on the porch outside.

Then amazingly, we finally fell into a bit of small talk by way of light relief. Thomas and Jeff discussed baseball and politics, while I silently processed what was about to be the biggest shift of my life to that point. I tried to stay with them in the room, rather than descend into self-centred reflection. I kept saying to myself, in a similar way to when I was hanging with Ronnie: *This is Thomas Banyacya, Keeper of the Prophecy . . . in real life! Stay awake for it!*

As we stood up to leave, Thomas took my upper arms in his hands and gazed deep into my eyes, all the way to my soul, searching from side to side and eventually settling on the left eye. 'Go away now and purify yourself, then you can help others. You will help many people.' Then he gave me a brief hug and we left.

Jeff dropped me off back at my motel. I walked in, flopped onto the bed face-down and proceeded to fall into a breakdown hole. It was like descending into blackness, deeper and deeper into nothingness: the nothingness of having no reference points, of having the superficial layers you mistook for you and your life penetrated by a shard of truth that makes little sense but which you know is more valid than anything going on in your thoughts.

Just like in the mini-episode in Wales that I described earlier, I was efficient and fast coming through this one. I lay falling into darkness for what seemed like an hour but which was probably no more than a few minutes, then hit what felt like the bottom – if you can imagine such a thing as the bottom of nothing – and thought, *Fuck this for a laugh: it's not going to get me anywhere fast, and if I'm meant to purify myself so I can help people, I'd better start at once.*

I got up, splashed cold water over my face and head, went up on the roof, and did tai chi in the moonlight, allowing in the notion of purification from cynicism and doubt in order to open the way to helping others. This was probably the first time I'd ever formed the intention to help others. As a concept, offering my services to people had never played large in my world schema. I'd always been happy to do so with energy healings, guided relaxation sessions, or any other ways that I could give. But I'd never actually formulated it as an intention, as a reason for doing whatever I was doing, as the thrust of my mission. I'd never created a sense of mission in the first place; I was just bumbling along doing what felt right at the time.

So as well as reinforcing the idea of being able to 'illusion' reality into a different shape by intending it so, Thomas initiated me on my mission to help the world, to be of service. And a short while later, incidentally, both sides dismantled a whole raft of missiles. The magic worked.

SONNY SPRUCE

For a long time I had to train myself to stop mixing Sonny with Sony – the power of branding ran deep even back in the late 1970s.

So I'd driven over the mountains from Santa Fe, seen Taos glistening in the distance with reflected sunlight at the foot of Taos Mountain, and pulled into a supermarket to buy a few provisions. Outside the store, I'd started chatting with a cool-looking young Indian dude drinking a can of beer in a pickup truck, with his shotgun nestled in its bracket against the rear windshield. He advised me

to head straight for the pueblo, a thousand-year-old pair
of adobe apartments built in pyramid shapes on either
side of the sacred river that ran down from Blue Lake.
So off I went and found myself following the sound of a
slow-tempo tom-tom drum, which I soon discovered was
being played by an old man in a small, dark, ground-floor
apartment in the pyramid on the river's east side.

He introduced himself as Old Man Frank and asked
me what I was doing there. I explained I was deeply
troubled by the state of the world and wanted to be
around an ancient culture with enough wisdom and
collective recall to teach me what I needed to know about
helping people in times of such upcoming, potentially
huge transitions (as we're witnessing now). In return,
I said that I'd share my own knowledge about tai chi,
meditation, yoga and so on. He laughed. He reminded
me a lot of both of my grandfathers rolled into one. He
told me to find Sonny Spruce, somehow intimating that
Sonny was a connection point for all crazed Anglos who
suddenly realise that there is more to understanding
reality than is generally assumed in the West (or had
watched too many episodes of *The Lone Ranger* as a kid
and had become enthralled by the romance and now just
wanted to hang out with Indians).

He told me to drive a mile back down the road until I
came to a house on the left, and I'd find him there.

There were no phones on the reservation back then
– not even landlines – so Old Man Frank had no way of

letting Sonny know that I was coming. Yet as I drove up, he was standing on his porch leaning back against one of the carved wooden support pillars, his arms crossed over his chest, as if he were waiting for me. I felt this so strongly that as I got out of the car, before even saying hello or introducing myself, I blurted out: 'Did you know I was coming or something?'

'Yeah,' he answered semi-laconically and extremely slowly, as if to say, 'Of course, what else would you expect?'

'Hi, I'm Stephen,' I said as we shook hands.

'Yeah,' he said again like he knew already. 'Stephen. Ste-ph-en,' he repeated, extending the 'ph,' playing with the sound between his lips as if it were some sort of phonic novelty. 'What are you doing here?'

Itinerant Englishmen weren't so common in the area then, especially ones like me. These days the place is well visited and has acquired that theme-park sheen, as have equivalent 'tribal' spots all over the world. But back then, other than a few adventurous French and Russian artists, the odd New York heiress, D.H. Lawrence, and a bunch of hippies from the Bay Area, not so many Englishmen made their way to Sonny's house.

I told him I was already mixing up Sonny with Sony in my head and laughed. He looked at me strangely as if he'd never heard anyone say anything as odd as that and chuckled. He'd never linked the two before and the notion seemed to amuse him. 'Walk-man!' He laughed at the ambiguity and headed into the house gesturing for me to follow. 'Come in.'

It was a humble yet perfectly appointed adobe home, and quite big by Indian standards at the time. The main room was sunken. The floor was made of compacted mud with flecks of straw, all glazed over and dark-coloured. The walls were painted white on the inside and were about two feet thick in most places: solid mud and straw that would withstand any onslaught by the elements. There were no sharp edges; everything was rounded. In one corner there was a fireplace with a rounded opening like the door of an igloo. On the walls were various pieces of Indian art, dreamweavers, feathers, tomahawks, and various sand-painting-style mandalas.

Sonny wore his hair in two braids, finely wrapped in colorful strands of cotton. He was one of the most handsome men I'd ever seen. His eyes shone like two fireballs of white light from a well-sculpted face with a square jaw and symmetrical yet craggy features. Like most of the guys in the tribe (no matter how traditional they were), he ironically wore the conventional cowboy costume, complete with boots, concha belt, tight Levi's, plaid shirt and leather vest, bolo tie with a silver clasp, and a plethora of silver and turquoise jewellery.

He was, and remains, by far and away the most grounded, centred person I'd ever met, even beyond my most influential martial-arts teachers. It was as if he and the earth were one, not just theoretically, not just as some fanciful New Age concept or visualisation, but palpably. In his presence, I felt the power of the earth, of all the ancestors from this planet and before. His being was profound.

There was never any question whether we were going to be friends. We were instantly so – brothers recognising each other after lifetimes, in spite of the unlikely guises we were each in now: the comparatively neurotic, post-hippie city boy from London and the timeless Indian warrior standing at 7,500 feet above sea level on the eastern edge of the Colorado Plateau with the piercing white light of the northern New Mexico sun shining everything up in sharp relief.

'What are you going to do here?' he asked as if there was no question that I was going to be invited to live the dream.

'I'm going to teach tai chi.'

'What's that?'

'It's a martial art from the land of the forefathers,' I said smiling, referring to the common origins of the Native Americans and the people of the Orient. 'It's from Taoism. Tai chi is an internal martial art that's practised slowly as a form of meditation, but with time it's a powerful method of self-defence.' I explained it excitedly and showed him a few moves.

He stood there looking at me amused, this bizarre example of modern humanity at its quirkiest (the likes of which he'd never seen before) demonstrating this even stranger and more bizarre form of slow-motion air boxing.

'I don't need to learn that shit!' he exclaimed, watching me carefully and laughing. I looked at him and instantly got his point, seeing how immensely grounded and contained his own *chi* was.

'Yeah, but I need to learn *that* shit!' I laughed and gestured to the way he stood there solid as a mountain.

And that's how it began: the quirky Englishman, the groovy Indian, and a friendship that would take me through a personal transformation so huge that I'm still feeling the effects of it to this day.

Sonny was one of the main dancers in the tribe. For the Tewa tribes, which are part of the greater Hopi nation, dance is one of the more powerful forms of communing with the Great Spirit, and not just a form of self-expression for a bit of a laugh or to let your hair down. Sonny related quite deeply to my tai chi, which for him was my equivalent. He never attempted to turn me into a Native American. Implicit in the subtext of our rapport was an understanding that he was helping me find my own power through my own methods, rather than teaching me to be like him. However, this wasn't conscious in me at the time – it was a process of becoming.

There was something about Sonny that made being around him always feel like an immense honour, like hanging out with a king of some vast nation. When I was

with him, I generally found myself behaving as I might
if I were going to receive a knighthood. It wasn't like
I was always on my best behaviour, but there was an
implied protocol and a huge respect for personal space,
which included no crowding of the other's mind with idle
chatter.

This made conversing awkward at times, yet it was
this very awkwardness that made the love so sweet
and poignant. When you don't have common cultural
references to draw your humour from, and when the
references you do have are so profound as to be nothing
short of cosmic, you have to be prepared to sit through
the discomfort of not knowing what to say to each other
for the first half hour every time you meet. And you have
to trust each other on a deep, animal level.

We humans use chatter as a defence behind which to
hide while we ascertain whether or not we're safe with
one another. But without recourse to this device, Sonny
and I had to sit through the initial discomfort like a pair of
wild animals and trust.

However, the pay-off for this trust was invariably
huge. I'd visit him three or four times a week, and we'd
sometimes walk around the pueblo to visit various people
or wander in the hills and mountains. Other times we'd
go out for a drive, sit in his kitchen, or often just stand on
his porch gazing out at the view for hours on end.

Once, I rolled up and he was standing on the porch,
leaning on the wall, his gaze fixed far into the distance at

the western range of the Rockies across the mesa. The sun was going down behind them, glowing pink like a blood orange, casting the fabled crimson light on the eastern spur that gives them their name: Sangre de Cristo (Blood of Christ).

'Hi, man.' He didn't answer. He just smiled with his eyes straight ahead, nodded slightly, and carried on gazing. I joined him, leaning against the wall looking out westward. It was an astonishing view – especially for someone more used to standing on Primrose Hill looking down at St. Paul's Cathedral in London – and one that never failed to stop me in my tracks.

I was fully stopped. I stood in silence and awe, watching the sun go down and the head of a storm blow in slowly from the west. The contrast symbolised the meta-paradox, the great yin and yang of existence. It didn't need verbalising – that would have been crass. After ten minutes or so, still with his eyes focused on the far view, Sonny said, 'Nowhere like northern New Mexico,' as if it were the most incontrovertible fact in existence. He wasn't asking for a response; no agreement was required. It was obvious anyway. I continued standing there in silence.

After another ten minutes, with my eyes still fixed on the far view, I said, 'No. Nowhere like it.'

This was a key moment. It had taken two years of meeting a few times a week for us to feel comfortable enough with each other that we were able to stand in total silence for so long. Nothing was said about it. That too would have been crass, but it was evidently noted by both of us. Sonny celebrated it by telling me the most outlandish story I'd ever heard.

Sonny was similar to Ronnie Laing in this respect. Ronnie had once told me a story about a friend of his who was a famous parapsychologist in Rio de Janeiro. This man had been experimenting on developing a doppelgänger and had been so successful that he was able to send this psychic clone of himself out to make love with his mistress, while he remained in bed making love to his wife.

The next morning he'd receive compliments on his sexual prowess from both wife and mistress, who would also each call him at the office later in the day to thank him for a great night. When Ronnie had finished the tale, he asked in his most mischievous Scottish accent, 'Do you believe that?'

'Yes . . . no . . . I don't know . . . no . . . yes . . . I don't know . . . yes,' I answered, hedging my bets and drawing no conclusion.

Sonny's tale that day was about a powerful, well-known *brujo,* or sorcerer, quite common in those parts. This man wanted his woman back after she had been seduced away by another younger *brujo*. This new guy had given her a silver ring and told her never to take it off or the bond of their love would break, and he'd no longer be able to protect her against the wrath of her former lover. One full-moon night, the older, more powerful *brujo* conjured the light of the moon into a focused beam that he directed at the window of the woman's bedroom, causing it to stream in, bounce off a mirror, and shine directly on the ring she wore on her finger. It was so powerful that the ring melted, thus breaking the protective field around her, and within 24 hours she was back living with him.

'Do you believe that?' Sonny asked in exactly the same mischievous tone as Ronnie, as if they were the same actor in different disguises.

'Yes . . . no . . . I don't know . . . no . . . yes . . . I don't know . . . yes,' I found myself stammering in more or less exactly the same way.

When we first met, I used to ask Sonny about the spiritual ways of the tribe, but it's not like talking to an anthropologist – that is, you don't get a summary. Instead, he would tell me stories, and within these would be snippets of information that would open up a whole new understanding in me. For instance, it was the way of the tribe in those days to have a meeting once a month. Everyone sat in a large circle, and one by one each participant would air their petty grievances with other members of the tribe. The individual who was being targeted would not respond or defend him- or herself, but would merely sit and take it in.

This had the effect of clearing the air on a social and practical level; for no matter how much you're able to witness the Great Spirit informing your fellows, when you live together, you get on each other's nerves from time to time and do things that piss each other off.

My talks with Sonny were interspersed with the occasional field trip. These were the treats – the bits I'd imagined in the Carlos Castaneda-style fantasy I'd had before setting off from London, and here they were happening before my very eyes: 'appointments with power', as Castaneda called them.

One night, under a full moon, we went for a walk in a dry arroyo down the canyon to the east of the reservation. The glaring white moonlight was brighter than ten stacks of LED stage lighting; every strand of sagebrush, every leaf on every plant, and every rock and pebble stood in stark contrast to whatever was around it. There was something altered-state-like about it without having to take drugs of any kind. Dotted about the place were plants with yellow flowers. Sonny took a knife and slit the stem of one, and dark viscous fluid oozed out. He took a drop on his finger, licked it, and gestured for me to do the same, as he continued to walk ahead in silence.

'What is it?'

'Like opium. Good for visions,' he answered after a while.

Half an hour later, I was communing with spirits and dancing in energy patterns – in a softer way, though, than would be induced by LSD or even mushrooms. It was more natural, a you'd-hardly-notice-it-if-you-weren't-paying-attention mild mescaline sort of high. No words passed between us, yet I was in full conversation with Sonny, or rather he with me, about the ancestors and how important it is to speak with them often, and if you do, they'll protect you and sort things out for you from the other side.

This was all going on in my head as far as I knew, yet it felt as real as steel.

The walk continued in silence for a while, and eventually we went back to our vehicles and said good night. The next time I saw him, he asked me if I remembered what he'd been telling me about the ancestors, as if it had been spoken out loud.

During the first Thanksgiving dinner at Sonny's house with his girlfriend, his young son, his mother and her husband, I asked whether they felt there was any irony in giving thanks for having their land stolen by the Anglos. Sonny was gracious about it: 'The Europeans have brought us many benefits. The Great Spirit brought them to us. We give thanks to the Great Spirit for that.'

The power in the municipality of Taos (on the informal, social-spiritual plane at least) was shared by the unofficial leaders of the Indian, Chicano, and hippie communities, respectively. The balance of power and keeping it steady seemed to depend on these three guys who met each evening for a drink at El Rincón, a traditional bar in the old Spanish-built town a couple of miles from the pueblo. You'd find at least two of them in there most evenings.

Sonny was the unofficial, but undisputed, leader of the Indian community.

The day I finally left to return to the UK, I stopped by that bar with an extremely heavy heart to say good-bye to Sonny. We were both quite moved – almost to tears – but not wanting to get soppy on each other, we didn't speak much, as usual. The silver bracelet on Sonny's wrist, one that I'd always admired for its elegant simplicity, was glowing with an extra-special light. As it glinted and caught my eye, he took it off his wrist – I'd never seen him take it off; it was a part of his arm, in my view – and put it on my wrist. 'This will protect you in the madness out there. Never take it off.' And I never have.

If I had to sum up what Sonny taught me, it was to pray and have awareness of the Tao, the Great Spirit, at all times and to know that the truth doesn't have to be spoken – you can feel it. But more important than that, it was to be myself.

One day after knowing Sonny for two years or so, I had a major revelation in that respect. It occurred to me as I was walking toward the mountain in the morning for my daily conversation with the Tao, when out of the blue, the Tao told me: 'You're not an Indian, you know!'

While this would be obvious to most people, to me it was one of the most profound realisations of my life so far. I wasn't an Indian. And I didn't need to try and be one or live like one. I just needed to be myself to stand in good relation to everyone and everything, and enjoy a beautiful life.

'Hey, man!' I walked into his house shouting like a lunatic. 'I'm *not* an Indian! Would you believe it? I only just got it. You know what I mean? I'm not an Indian and that's okay!'

He got it. He didn't say anything but just smiled. He'd been waiting for me to see it and say it. It was at that point that our friendship deepened and he started revealing his secrets to me, which you may have noticed I haven't told you. And do you know why? Because they're secrets.

JOE SWASSO

Joe Swasso was the medicine man, mending people with his bare hands and his magic. Because of my friendship with Sonny, he agreed to teach me some moves. I learned the technique of Indian massage, which is extraordinarily similar to the Taoist style except that the Indians refer to muscle lines, while the Taoists consider them to be energy channels.

As Joe worked, he chanted softly to the Great Spirit, as if his kneading along the muscle lines was a way of opening his patients' bodies to the Great Spirit's healing power. He burned sage to purify everyone and said prayers on behalf of his patients in order to restore harmony between them and the powers of the four directions, the Earth, and the Great Spirit as it expresses itself through the people and things of the world. I know this, not because he took the time to explain it to me, but because that's how it felt. And when I described it to him in this way, he agreed that my explanation was correct. He wasn't teaching a course; he was sharing from the heart and soul. He wasn't presenting information; he was allowing me into a secret world of subtle power. That's the way it works with Native Americans. It's totally different from us, with our courses and systems and slick explanations for mass consumption.

Joe used what he called *coyote medicine,* meaning that he was a bit of a trickster. He told me that I was too. He implied with hand gestures and facial expressions that most conditions affecting the body were psychogenic and could be removed by getting into the mind. Another reason for his chanting was to create a trance-inducing rhythm so he could establish a moment of unity between him, the patient (and me, when I was present), and the Great Spirit, in its unseen form and its manifest form as you and me.

Again, this is my interpretation, and it's essentially a subjective one, tempered by the experiences taken in by my senses, through a filter of my own making, composed of what I wanted to see. Still, I'd bet on it being the same impression most informed onlookers would have felt too.

While my dealings with Joe were fairly infrequent, my innate understanding of the shamanistic tools of rhythm, trance induction, and physical stimulus was profoundly fed by them.

OLD JOE SUNHAWK

Every morning at around 11, Old Joe Sunhawk would stand outside the barber shop in the town plaza, like the old guru available for an informal *satsang*. Old Joe was none other than Geronimo's grandson and well into his 90s, yet he was still upright and fit as a fiddle, as sharp-eyed as a hawk on the wing, and as bright and luminescent as the midday sun.

Geronimo has always been a prominent icon of warriorhood and courage for me, ever since my war cry as a boy: *'Geronimooooooo!'* So standing with his grandson – who was old enough to be my great-great-grandfather – always seemed a little like standing with a pharaoh or someone slightly otherworldly, a denizen of the realm of myth. I'd have, at such times, an imaginary audience and me, saying: *Well, look at me standing with Geronimo's grandson. Check me out with my friend Old Joe Sunhawk! Have you ever known someone with a name like that who also happened to be Geronimo's grandson?!* And I guess the audience would applaud and let out a collective *Wow!* . . . And then I'd return to standing there being with Old Joe.

Like Thomas Banyacya, Old Joe was concerned about the world and would talk to me about it. I was a novelty to him, as I was to all the Native Americans there. Quirky English eccentrics sporting long hair and beards, talking too quickly (like Jesus on speed) and wearing mountain-man dungarees and moccasins wasn't something they came across very often in those days. Old Joe was concerned about the young ones and the way they had no values. He was primarily referring to the tribe, but meant all of us by extension. To the Indian fathers like him, the tribe was at the centre of the universe, and everyone around was a reflection of what went on in the tribe, so if there was disharmony or greed present, it would by extension affect all of the world in time. And how right he was.

He talked about the necessity of walking lightly on the ground, because that was the mantle of Mother Earth. He talked about the absurdity of people thinking they could own bits of it. He talked about the uranium mining west of there and how that would destabilise the whole planet. And he talked about the need to be around the people you love when the world starts rocking and rolling as he expected it would anytime now.

But most of all, he talked silently through his eyes, of unfathomable wisdom and light; and from his heart, love poured forth so that standing with him in the plaza for 20 minutes was like being blessed by Grandfather Universe himself.

As well as confirming the teachings for me, he also showed me by his very presence that those who serve as your icons can actually become part of your real life. And if not them, then their grandsons may do so, which is almost as potent a symbol of manifesting, and which beautifully illustrates how all this is possible because the whole show is merely a dream in the mind of the Tao.

*** ***

Chapter Nine

Rounding Off the Training

I don't know if you've ever had the experience of sitting in front of someone who transmogrifies (that is, shape-shifts) from a man to a woman, to an old woman, to an old man, to a young boy, to an old master, and back into his original form in a fluid motion – as if you're watching all of this person's reincarnations play out at once. Well, I experienced this while sitting in a small auditorium in Taos one evening back in 1980, watching spiritual teacher and author Ram Dass giving his talk for the first time.

RAM DASS

It was the exact same lecture that I saw Ram Dass give subsequently over and over again (almost word for word) in many different settings around the world, yet always with the same inspiring enthusiasm and authenticity. This is a distinctly American oratory talent I have great admiration for, as I find it hard to be authentic myself if attempting to recite from some sort of mental script; and so am obliged to improvise my way through every talk I do to keep it absolutely fresh in style, content and approach.

Ram Dass, however, had quite a story to tell – having been at the forefront of the intimately related but subtly distinct realms between psychedelia and spirituality – so it was worth having it down pat; and it never failed to impress me, other than on one occasion when I mistakenly had a go at him about being inauthentic (but more about that later).

So there I was a mile and a half above sea level in the mountain desert with a couple of hundred other people, thinking (probably mildly histrionically) that he was doing this whole thing specifically for me. As I watched his face change from one archetype to the next and back again, I found myself transfixed by his story, feeling an overwhelming sensation of love in my heart. So strong was it that had I been given to following gurus, I was certain I would have left everything there and then and followed him to the ends of the earth. However, I knew that wouldn't be the case; I was meant to forge my own path as a guru, no matter how appealing following another might have felt in the moment.

And I felt the need to share this with him.

So after the talk I went up to him, and as our eyes met, Ram Dass smiled in recognition. I hadn't been imagining it! It turned out that he actually *had* been looking at me, addressing me directly throughout most of the lecture. He spontaneously put the back of his hand on the centre of my chest as we stood there, and moved it around in small circles as if unlocking my heart centre. I could feel it working while we stood there smiling at each other from spirit to spirit, Krishna saying hello to himself.

'You know, I'd never follow anyone. It's not in my nature. I know I have my own path to follow,' I said. 'But if I were ever going to follow anyone, it would be you. You are absolutely divinely beautiful at the deepest and highest level.'

He smiled in total understanding and hugged me warmly. 'Let's stay in touch,' he suggested, and gave me his contact details.

This led to a series of meetings all over the place, in group settings and in private. We met once in London, once in Tuscany, again in Taos when I was back there on a visit, and once in Switzerland. It was there, high up in the Swiss mountains, that I challenged him about him being fake, always repeating the same story, not calling himself by his real name, and so on.

It happened at a ceremony as people were bowing at his feet. The sight of all that guru worship had gotten to me. I jumped to my feet, ignoring the line of people waiting to speak to him, and strode right up and planted myself before him on the dais. 'I'm getting really pissed off at you!' I exclaimed. 'You're so full of shit with all this guru nonsense—' But as I was ranting, I was looking into his eyes, which were totally clear of any trace of ego, perfectly humble and compassionate, open and expressing love and the divine presence. I just as suddenly stopped. 'I realise . . .' I started, my eyes filling with tears, 'that I'm talking about myself. I see my own reflection in your eyes and realise that it's *me* I'm pissed off at.'

That was one of the quickest resolutions I'd ever known.

'No, go on,' he said. 'I'd really like to know more about it.' So we fell into a discussion about his name. He explained that for him, Richard Alpert (his birth name) was no more. Since initiation with his guru, he had died to that former self. We also talked about the way he always stuck to a set script. "The script is just a form. The real transmission comes from here," he stated and once again placed the back of his hand on my chest.

'I know,' I said. And we hugged.

Another time we met in Italy, where he was teaching a workshop and I was, coincidentally, in the region. I dropped by to see him for afternoon tea. Sitting outside in the Tuscan countryside, we began discussing my future as a spiritual teacher. He warned me that after years of constantly working to get the world to hear your message, when at last everyone finally catches on to what you're offering, the pressure is daunting. Everyone wants a bit of you; everyone wants you to heal them, to take their pain away. And if you're not careful, if you don't ensure you get adequate time alone with Spirit in which to restore yourself, the pressure can destroy you, as it so cruelly almost did him by way of a stroke in his later life.

If I had to define what I learned from Ram Dass over the years we were in contact, I'd say that, in a word, it was *love* – the love occurring when the chest is soft and the mind is willing to share. Love is the key to reality working. Second, he taught me that we're here merely so that Spirit can act out on the Earth plane through us: each of us is really the divine in disguise, coming to meet each other (Spirit saying hello to itself is one of our highest functions). Third, we're able to live simultaneously on the spiritual plane – via the centre brain region, where everything (including all the world's suffering) is perfect as it is – and on the human plane (via the heart centre, where the pain of it all truly sucks).

It's this paradox and the ability to accommodate it with equanimity and compassion, without feeling the need to try in vain to resolve it, that's crucial to successfully negotiating our way through the game of life on all levels. It keeps our mind, body and spirit working on some semblance of unity in relation to itself and the outside world so that we can do everything possible to help alleviate suffering wherever and whenever. And if we enter every situation with the question 'How can I serve here?' rather than 'How can this serve me?' things work out for us far better.

Finally, I learned that we exist on the local plane by virtue of the melodramas we create in our minds. There's nothing we can do about them other than to have compassion for ourselves as we observe them playing out. This aspect of us that bears witness is who we really are, and that is the one being informing all of us. And it's okay to simplify it and call that being Love.

TELL US GOOD MORNING

Tell Us Good Morning owned a drum shop on the road to the pueblo where he made and sold the finest Indian tom-tom drums on the planet, but his real function seemed to be to transmit positive energy to those who might be feeling sorry for themselves or be a bit down on any given day. The game was that one would swing by his place in the morning, where he'd usually be sitting on his porch, and say, 'Hello, Tell Us Good Morning.'

He'd smile from the bottom of his heart, from the bottom of the heart of the whole universe, from ear to ear, as if lighting up the sky itself, and simply reply, 'Good

Moorrrrning!' with the emphasis on the '*orn.*' This would invariably fill me (or whoever else he was saying it to) with absolute glee just for being alive.

If you went by any other time of day, he was usually inside, so you didn't get a chance to speak to him unless you wanted to disturb him. However, if you did meet him at some other time, the protocol was to call him *Tell Us,* as in: 'Hi, Tell Us.'

He'd sometimes respond with a 'Tell you what?' and burst out laughing. Tell Us taught me the raw, naked joy of being alive simply because I'm alive. And I learned that however everyday life is shaping up, no matter how serious your personal melodrama appears, it's not so serious that you can't still feel that innate joy of being alive somewhere deep inside.

AL HUANG

In those days, Al Huang (the author of the modern tai chi classic *Embrace Tiger, Return to Mountain* and one of the finest exponents and masters of the practice who was ever born) used to run five-week residential sessions in some of the world's most beautiful places. Participants would come from all parts of the globe and pay a handsome sum in order to learn his basic tai chi form, gain a true understanding of the joys of the practice and even pick up a few calligraphic skills in to the bargain.

One year Al came to Taos and set up camp at a fancy venue at the foot of the mountains. Once word got out that he was in town, I started riding my bike through the sagebrush each afternoon to where he was staying, and I'd sit on the ground and watch him go through his solo practice under a tree. He'd transit from one posture to the next seamlessly, so it was like watching someone in motion without being able to see the actual movement.

For a couple of days, I sat patiently under a cottonwood tree a hundred feet or so away – distant, entranced, and thinking that he hadn't spotted me. I didn't want to disturb him. But after he'd finished on the second day, he slowly came toward me. It was like witnessing an apparition. Again, without my spotting any visible motion, he was suddenly standing in front of me.

'Hi, I'm Stephen. I didn't want to disturb you – I just wanted to watch you. I've never seen anything as beautiful as your tai chi.' We shook hands warmly. I explained that I was the local tai chi teacher, and we fell into a long conversation. He told me some of his life story, how he'd been learning tai chi in China since he was six, had become a dancer in San Francisco, and had understood that tai chi was the dance of eternal joy. Indeed, I was all but overcome by the innate happiness he expressed in his tone, his eyes, his body language and his smile: he was pure joy in motion.

Al invited me to come back each day to watch him practise. We engaged in some in-depth discussions about *chi* and how it moves, and how joy is the greatest motivator of people and society – and affirmed that we must do all that we can to promote joy in everything we do, as only that will save the world from itself.

I persuaded him to come into town one night and do a session in the old plaza for my students. He duly came along with his bamboo flute and taught about 50 of us a short five-elements form, playing his flute all the while. It was without a doubt one of the most magical happenings I've ever been a part of, with the local police driving slowly around the plaza in open-mouthed astonishment as a large number of people moved their arms slowly and joyfully in the evening air to the sound of this tai chi Pied Piper's bamboo flute.

I was high off that for months, even years afterwards, and the joy Al imparted still stays with me every day as I practise the form.

PSYCHO DAN

Psycho Dan was on the run, hiding out in the mountains from a Chinese gang in New York after pulling someone's ears off with his bare hands (using a technique charmingly called *wind-dried ears,* or so he said). He had a wispy moustache, a mad stare in his eyes and a face so bristling with latent psychotic emotion that his features seemed to be constantly twitching.

How we became friends I don't recall, but he utterly fascinated me. I'd heard that he was an expert in tai chi 'combat', something extremely rare in those days. I wanted to learn it with a lust so powerful that nothing would have stopped me from connecting with Dan, no matter how much of a loose cannon he was purported to be.

So a couple of times a week, we'd meet at the foot of the mountain and he'd kick the shit out of me. He'd show me a technique once, but before I'd even had time to process it, he'd attack me and expect me to use what he'd just briefly demonstrated, against him. It was a brutal way of teaching, yet it worked.

Gradually, over the months, I was able to field most attacks with a degree of competence, other than the occasional surprise heel-kick down on top of my head, which seemed to come out of nowhere and would leave me dazed and stunned for hours afterwards. Miraculously, he never seriously injured me, and I like to put this down to some innate compassion and mastery on his part, although it was probably just luck on my part and, no doubt, a host of angels protecting me.

After six months or so, Dan was set to leave town. By then I pretty much knew how to handle myself in a combative situation. He looked me in the eyes, his moustache twitching, his eyebrows darting hither and thither, and fixed me with an intense gaze as if he were about to rip *my* ears off. Then he asked one of the weird,

other being *pa kua,* which he told me he also practised).
I'd heard of pa kua because some dude known as Master
Li had lived to be 287 years old (which was chronicled
in *The New York Times*), mostly on account of his pa
kua practice. I'd always wanted to learn it so I could live
that long too but I hadn't yet heard of Hsing I. It was like
how it must be with some people who suddenly take to
wanting to own a Ferrari with all their heart, soul and
might the first time they merely hear the word *Ferrari*.
That's how quickly I came to want to learn Hsing I.

I all but begged Bobby to teach me. He agreed, and
there ensued a year or so of me studying Hsing I and pa
kua with him twice a week. What I learned from him – as
well as undoubtedly two of the most wonderful boxing
systems known to humankind – was the ability to be silent
around my practice, rather than talking a load of shit just
for the sake of it each time I came back into the everyday
state. This occurred from him teaching me the moves, and
me doing them and feeling as if I were flying. I wanted
to blurt out how amazing it all was, but somehow I was
unable to speak in my exhilarated state. He spotted it fully
and laughed the first time – in such a way as if to say there
really was no need to speak, and there was nothing one
could say anyway, as what we were doing was ineffable.

However, he did impart a crucial piece of information
to me, one that has placed me in good stead ever since:
when dealing with opponents, whether actually or
metaphorically, the key to remaining in command of

yourself and the situation (the way to attune to what they're intending and thus be prepared with a viable defence) is to listen to their energy. It's inaudible, but you can still 'hear' their intention moving in this or that direction. And the way to sensitise yourself to this level of ability is to listen behind you. It doesn't make sense to the rational mind, but try it and you'll instantly know what I mean. Listen *behind you,* and you'll perceive an instant expansion of your peripheral awareness.

Here was yet another instance of how sound was connected to everything I was doing – even if it was the inaudible sound (or sacred *shabd*) of the Tao, moving its intention in various ways and in the form of an apparent opponent blocking your path.

Other than that, Bobby showed me how to move the *chi* through my joints and along my limbs in a way that I'm grateful for every day as I do my practice. But his real gift was the deep understanding that words are irrelevant . . . and that's ironic, considering that I make my living with words.

DAN SANTOS

Dan Santos had come from the Bay Area with the first wave of hippies arriving in New Mexico in the late 1960s to set up communes. He was descended from a Taoist lineage with roots in Macao, and was practising acupuncture near Santa Fe. We met one day at a tai chi convention hosted by Ben Lo, one of Cheng Man Ching's students from San Francisco, and were paired off in the pushing-hands exercises. Two people couldn't have been more different on the surface, yet more similar deep down, than he and I: Dan was slight, dark, subtle and mysterious with his Asian-Portuguese looks; and I was cruder – English, gawky and vaguely urban neurotic . . . albeit right there with the *chi*.

I explained that I was considering returning to the UK to study acupuncture. I'd met the Japanese master in Santa Fe, and although I'd liked him a lot, I didn't really want to learn Japanese-style acupuncture. I would have much rather studied with the Chinese master there but had heard that he only took on a couple of apprentices at a time and was completely full for years on that front.

Dan didn't say anything about it; he just listened as we continued the push hands. He evidently appreciated my grasp on the *chi*, for as we said goodbye at the end, he slipped me his business card and told me to visit him on the following Wednesday morning. It wasn't until I got into my car that I looked closely at the card and realised that he was the Chinese master I'd wanted to study with.

Nice move on his part – subtle, as with everything else he did, as it turned out.

For me, on the other hand, it instigated three days of wondering and worrying: could he have meant that he was inviting me to be a student, or was he just planning to give me some advice about going back to the UK? In those days, I often found myself stressing over my possible options. I still do so occasionally, but back then it was a major pastime, winding myself up with the I-Ching, a pendulum (used in divination), or a tarot deck to help the madness along.

So when I got to Santa Fe that Wednesday at 11 A.M. as requested, I was relieved, stunned, overjoyed, flattered, taken aback, and brought sharply and humbly into the present moment, when I found him standing on a chair attempting to fix a patient/cubicle-divider curtain that had come loose from the rail. All he said was: 'Pull the other end of this cord.' I did and we stood together for a moment in silence, looking at the now-fixed cubicle.

'Now, I want you standing behind me at all times,' he finally said, without even questioning whether I wanted to be his apprentice, or letting me know that he'd decided to take me on as one. 'When I turn left, you turn left behind me – I don't want to know you're there. Watch everything I do. You can ask me questions at lunchtime and at the end of the day. If I ask you to hold or pass needles to me, do so without a word. *I don't want to know you're there.* If I ask you a question, answer in one or two words. This will teach you the real meaning of investing in loss. I want you to reach a stage where you don't even know you're here yourself. Okay?'

'Okay,' I agreed, slightly bemused but resonating with this picture fully.

'I'll give you notes to study at night and test you on those as we go along. These are *my* notes – you won't find anything similar to them in the whole world. Okay?'

'Okay.'

The first morning, I shuffled about behind him looking over his shoulder as he went from cubicle to cubicle taking pulses, placing his hands on patients to issue *chi*, and inserting pins with great subtlety. I tried to think of a good question, but because he explained to each patient precisely what he was doing and why – possibly for my benefit, possibly for the patient's, possibly for his – he answered all my questions.

At lunch, I pointed out how I'd noticed that he tended to use the same set of ten or so points in varying orders and asked why he didn't use more of the thousand or so points available. He explained that these were the ten most powerful ones – the rest were just for showing off. If I could learn to use even one of these points properly, fully and effectively in the course of my lifetime, I'd be doing well. Meanwhile, Dan told me that he was going to teach me these ten points so I knew them better than the back of my hand. Then I asked him if the point he was using below each knee was stomach 36 or gall bladder 34.

'I won't answer questions like that. If you want me to answer a question, phrase it differently. For example, ask "Is that stomach 36?" and I'll say "No, stupid, that's gall bladder 34." Get it?'

'Got it!' I replied, laughing.

He didn't laugh, but his eyes were always smiling anyway, which spontaneously elicited a tone of mild kidding around on my part in order to counter his bizarre approach to teaching me. I noticed that he made a point of cracking light gags with every patient, invariably making them laugh a fair bit during a treatment.

'You seem to make everyone laugh,' I said at the end of day two, eager to come up with a good question yet thinking that I was dredging the bottom of the barrel. 'Why is that? To amuse yourself?'

'That's probably the most important question you'll ever ask me,' he replied. 'Laughter is the most powerful medicine of all. The needles, the healing – all of it is just a dance compared to laughter. You won't be graduating from here until I hear you making patients laugh, so you'd best brush up on your jokes.'

As it happens, I've always been crap at remembering jokes but do possess a bit of a talent for turning a situation on its head in a *Monty Python*-esque, Dadaist sort of way, and so give rise to mirth in those I encounter. I naturally fell into this approach. As time went by, Dan left me alone with patients more often, with instructions to keep my hands on their head, chest or belly (wherever he deemed appropriate to ensure an optimised healing effect of his acupuncture, and also because of the depths I was going to with the home-study aspect of the training). I found myself growing more and more contemplative.

One day a number of Tibetan monks who'd walked all the way around the world for peace arrived in Santa Fe. They came into the clinic and deposited what I took to be the youngest of their group for treatment for a respiratory complaint. Once the needles had been inserted, I was left alone with this monk, and was instructed to keep my palms flat on his breastbone and transmit *chi* by breathing along my arms through my palms and thinking white light.

It suddenly dawned on me that rather than stand there like a mere technician, I was at liberty to feel the natural, innate human kindness within and impart that along with the *chi*. It was a major revelation that medicine of any kind was all about love – that is, transmitting love and kindness to the other. I'm sure this message came straight out of the monk's heart centre; as if that was the message he'd been sent to bring me.

Interestingly, at that point I looked more closely at the patient who I'd thought was a teenaged monk, and realised he was about 70. I started telling him how I was amazed by his strength to walk so long and far, and asked him if he ever wondered why he was doing it, and whether it would really make a difference. Somehow or other our conversation turned humorous, and he was soon gleefully chuckling.

Dan walked in, smiled, and said approvingly, 'Very good.' This was the first compliment he'd paid me, and it was like receiving a medal. I've always wished I could be like that with my own students so that my positive comments to them would really pack the intended punch, but I tend to get so excited at the slightest sign of progress that I simply can't hold it back right from the start.

During lunch that day, I asked, 'So, is this all really about love, transmitting loving-kindness to the patient? Is that what does the healing?'

Dan then recounted the Zen-monk story: a novice goes to the abbot after a few months of meditation and, all excited, tells the abbot how through his meditation practice he's been enjoying the most amazing visions of the nine celestial spheres and how these have been revealing the secrets of life to him. The old monk looks at him and says, 'Just keep breathing. It will pass.' Dan explained that I was being overly sentimental and should concentrate on the *chi*, but he put it warmly, as if to acknowledge that I really was right on some level.

If I occasionally failed in containing my personality and was taking up too much psychic space in the room, Dan would put me on herb-mixing duty. This entailed standing for ages, mixing up bits of strange herbs into various formulas in order to resolve 'damp heat', tone 'kidney fire', dispel 'liver wind', and so on. I was as enchanted with the arcane translations of the Chinese as I was with the medicine itself. Dan knew that it was the needles that really grabbed me (I had an antipathy to the herbs, so he took pleasure in making me focus on them). It was like being in detention at school. One day I rebelled and blurted, 'I don't want to do the fucking herbs anymore! I think they're stupid! They make people have the weirdest reactions, and I don't like the smell.'

He just laughed.

The next day he started me on feeling the patients' pulses. This was a major breakthrough for me in my studies, as pulse reading is traditionally the primary method of making a feasible diagnosis and is considered to make up at least 97 per cent of the training in Oriental medicine. The protocol was that Dan would take the pulse on one side, and once he'd moved to the patient's other side to take the pulse there, I'd feel the pulse on the first side, then quickly walk to the other side to feel it there as well without getting in his way as he started inserting needles.

'What do you find?' he asked me.

'Kidney yin low; spleen soggy?'

'No. Kidney yang in excess.'

This went on for months. I was always wrong.

Let me explain a bit about Oriental pulse diagnosis just to put it in context. (If you're not interested, skip it and move to the next part of the story.)

There are three pulse positions on the radial artery along each wrist near the thumb. Placing your first three fingers with the forefinger flush with the base of the patient's palm and the ring finger toward the body enables you to 'hear' what's going on in that side of the patient around the kidneys, bladder, sexual organs, lower intestines and so on. The middle finger is feeling what's going on around the organs of digestion and blood production (stomach, spleen, pancreas, liver, gall bladder and so on), but on the other side of the body. So the right-hand pulse gives you a reading of the spleen on the left, and the left-hand pulse gives you a reading of the liver on the right. The forefingers, pushed up against the base of the palm, are getting a reading of the heart on the left wrist and the lungs on the right. That's at the deep level when you're pushing hard enough to all but cut the pulse off. At the superficial level, where you're pushing so lightly that you can hardly feel the beat, you're reading the bowels and brain.

The pulse is also described as having 28 distinct qualities, ranging from wiry to watermelon, which describe the actual sound of the beat, as it were.

Learning to differentiate between the 12 positions (3 deep and 3 superficial on each side) and the various strengths of pulse at each position, and then to identify the different sounds, is enough to induce a nervous breakdown in the hardiest of students.

Probably for this reason, these days many acupuncture schools (no doubt trying to reduce the student dropout rate) tend not to emphasise or even teach pulse reading. They rely more on tongue diagnosis, which is visual and far easier to interpret. And I can empathise with that. It doesn't, though, grant access to the patient's soul, and without this knowledge, the practitioner isn't able to have a proper look around to see what's happening at the deepest level.

It was my being a musician that finally helped. One day I was expressing my dismay at being so perplexed by the 28 sounds when Dan pointed to his ear said, 'Listen! Just listen! It's sound – it's not intellectual. *Just listen!*'

Suddenly I made the connection between the sounds of the pulse and the tones of a nice, fat bass note as if I were playing it on a bass guitar. When the sound is round and full, solid and clean, with a clear attack, and a healthy sustain and decay, it indicates perfect ingress, effective processing and assimilation, and efficient outflow of *chi* through that particular organ. The less perfect that note in solidity, fatness, attack, sustain, or decay, the less perfectly the *chi* is being processed by that organ along the respective phases. Plus, the kinds of qualities you feel that are less than perfect indicate either excess heat or excess cold in that organ, and so on.

I was truly going nuts over the pulses. I was obsessed with understanding them and was fairly desperate, because until then I'd only experienced getting it wrong, and I'd reached the stage of being utterly baffled.

That evening I drove back along the Rio Grande, the sun setting over the mountains to my left. As I crested the hill and saw the town of Taos twinkling in the distance, all at once I decided that I wasn't going to think about the pulses rationally any more. I never thought about music rationally; rather, I used all my primal instincts to feel it.

So I'd decided to rely upon those instincts and trust my skills in this faculty (whenever I wasn't driving myself mad with rational doubts or playing devil's advocate). I'd tell myself that I now totally got the pulses. I was big into the notion that I created my own reality, or the appearance of it, which was the big topic that everyone was talking about in those parts at the time. I was having a lot of metaphysical fun with the idea, so I thought I'd use some of that to now choose to be a master at reading the pulses.

So all the way back to Santa Fe the next morning, I pictured myself playing a nice, fat bass note on a bass guitar while telling myself over and over out loud: 'I now understand the pulses. I am a master pulse reader.'

I walked into the clinic with what must have looked like a halo around me. And wouldn't you believe it, from that moment on, instead of saying 'No, wrong' to my findings, Dan affirmed 'Yes, right!' and continued to do so from that day on.

That was proper magic. In some ways, this proof of how the mind creates reality was more important than anything in my training.

When teaching me the meditation from where all Taoist medicine originates, Dan erred on the side of pragmatism. The microcosmic orbit, or psychic loop, is at the core of Taoist meditation practice. This is when the mind and breath are led up the rear of the spine, pulling energy with them in a fine stream, over the top of the brain and down the front of the spine to between the legs, then back into the spine to start again. You do this a number of times in order to generate the shape and psychic form of the 'immortal spirit-body'; the vehicle that not only carries your consciousness intact to goodness knows where after physical death, but it also confers upon you superhuman manifesting, healing, and self-defence powers in this life.

These are essentially the skills that I've dedicated my life to teaching ever since I learned them myself. Developing the facility for turning the psychic loop efficiently in meditation practice is undoubtedly one of, if not the most, powerful metaphysical, alchemical devices I've ever encountered. When it came time to teach it to me, Dan was fully cognisant that I'd already been reading all about it in the notes, and all he said was, 'This will make you strong.'

But the way he said it, his tone, his facial expression and his eye twinkle transmitted the profound significance of practising this technique a thousand times more strongly than had he attempted to put it in words. Indeed, my propensity for rationally explaining or describing things to myself (and then to others), which in time led to my becoming a writer, was and remains anathema to the Taoist mind-set. Rather than explain something, the Taoist demonstrates it by showing you an exercise that moves the *chi* in such a way that you don't need any intellectual rationalisation.

But as Dan always remarked, this ancient Taoist stuff was forced out of China during the revolution in 1949. This caused the traditional practitioners who could afford it to flee to America, just so the Western mind with its developed, rational-mode intellect could act upon the ancient knowledge. The resulting fusion would reignite the original brilliance of the Taoist system. So on that score, Dan would be behind my shooting my mouth off about it as I tend to do. It certainly wasn't his way, though.

One day, quite a few years after I'd left, I went back to visit. As I walked up to the clinic, Dan came outside like he'd felt someone coming. (This is often the way in those parts, where the telepathic communication lines are so much more wide open than in busy cities.) He stopped for a moment in mild shock, as he hadn't been expecting me, then as recognition set in – this all took only a nanosecond – he approached and gave me the most wonderful, unprecedented hug. Then he held me away from him, looked deep into my eyes for a moment, deep within my soul, and said in an approving but jocular fashion complete with a fake redneck accent: 'Hell, you could do this stuff drunk now!'

'How about on acid?' I quipped.

Dan taught me a wealth of knowledge and skills in helping people overcome disease and get into a state of good health, which is nothing to sneeze at. But just as important, he ingrained into me the ability to look into someone's eyes, into their soul, and read precisely what's going on – thus avoiding a whole raft of wasted time talking bullshit because you're both too scared to get to the point. In time, I learned to do it without even looking into my patients' eyes – I could 'see' the problem just by scanning their aura. I got so slick at this over the years I was in practice healing people that I could accurately read their energy just from looking at them on the video display as they rolled up for their session. For although I say that reading the pulse the way Dan taught me is 97 per cent of the medicine, even that is only there to confirm what you already know by tuning in to a person's energy field.

If I had to boil down all the wisdom and knowledge Dan imparted to me, which is patently ridiculous, I'd say that it was the ability to allude to the opposite of what you're saying or not saying, and thus lead others' minds there far more effectively than by stating the obvious. It's the art of being oblique to gain a greater result than by going at it directly – a vital aspect of using the Taoist *wu-wei* effortless manifesting system, which I described in my earlier books *Manifesto* and *Pure*. I'm not sure that I've learned much of that skill, but it remains something to aspire to. Sometimes, too, you can gain far more by making people laugh than by forcing them into a serious stance when negotiating something, be it their healing or getting something you want.

And overall what strikes me now is again the connection between sound and healing, sound and existence, and sound and my work. Dan insisted that I had to listen to the pulse – that it was about sound – and that simple instruction opened up the door to the entire realm of diagnosing someone from the soul level up.

*** ***

Chapter Ten

The Tao's Deepening Effect

Govinda, with his flowing golden locks and deep-set steady gaze, was a hippie from Canada who had become a master of polarity therapy. Simply because he liked hanging out with me, he drove up from Santa Fe once a week for a whole year to teach me how to connect the body's various energy circuits and balance the flow of the yin and yang *chi* – mostly by pressing, or otherwise subtly manipulating, two polar opposite energy points simultaneously.

For instance, if you were treating a patient with lower-back pain, you'd place one finger on the epicentre of the pain and another on one of the ankles in order to create a circuit that would lead the blocked energy toward the extremities – and once there, it could be released through the toes. This corresponded with and complemented the Taoist approach, and also offered a few really nifty moves and holds that have informed the way I touch people ever since. It also addressed, in-depth, the idea of balancing the two sides of the brain and body in ways that the Taoist system doesn't, and so added to my overall understanding of how the mind-body-spirit complex works. Moreover, Govinda's spiritual practice was strong; being in his presence was a boon to the soul in itself.

Also his incredibly long, silky, golden hair fascinated me, as mine was curly, wavy and dark. However, coiffure notwithstanding, the most powerful thing I ever learned from him was to trust my ability to let my higher self take over – furthermore, trusting my higher self's ability to see me through even the most challenging situations.

This developed through his insistence that we meditate together before and after a training session. Then after the closing meditation, we discussed higher-self issues in more detail and described whatever experiences we'd had in the previous week in connection with it. Taos was like that in those days. Huge amounts of valuable knowledge were being shared or traded on an informal basis, but everyone took it very seriously and went about it all in a highly disciplined way. So an unusual rapport developed between us, quite unlike any other I'd known or have known since.

One day Govinda shared a story with me that indirectly – many years after – saved my life and, for a while longer at least, the life of one of my greatest, most startlingly arresting teachers of all: Frank Bernard Kramer (much more of him is soon to come).

Govinda had been teaching me the technique of closing my eyes and still being able to see the room around me by using my third eye in the midbrain. He was far more advanced in this than I was. One night he arrived and explained that he'd been really tired from being overly busy and not getting enough sleep. So he'd decided to drive the entire winding 60 miles or so along the Rio Grande (as it snakes through the foothills between Santa Fe and Taos) *with his eyes closed*. He did so partly so he could get some sleep and partly as an experiment, because by then he was feeling extremely confident in his midbrain viewing skills.

I tend toward scepticism by nature, yet I instinctively believed every word he said because his words resonated with truth throughout my body. (That's how you know when someone's lying: their words don't resonate in your belly properly.) At the end of the evening, for the sake of proving that I wasn't wrong to believe him, he drove off with his eyes closed (and a smile on his face). I watched him take a couple of potentially perilous bends near the house, and it was just as if he'd had his eyes open. Make of it what you will.

A few years later, I was driving Frank Kramer (as I mentioned, his story will follow a bit later) back from Cornwall to London after five days of non-stop revelry at Whirl-Y-Gig: the first and foremost alternative, post-hippie club night in the UK, specialising in ethnic beats and deep altered-state lighting and visual effects – generally, a wild night out. It was a bit like a Grateful Dead concert brought up-to-date with the intensity button firmly pressed on. Frank was the 'house philosopher', and I was the 'house doc'. The annual crew parties made the actual weekly club nights look quite tame in comparison, and I was so tired from all the fun, revelry, dancing and lack of sleep that I didn't even realise I'd fallen asleep while driving full speed on the motorway. However, one part of my mind was remembering Govinda and his great feat. So I went with it and was able to see the lane ahead through my forehead quite clearly (coloured a tad differently, though) and long enough to consciously draw myself back into the awake state and open my eyes. Frank told me that my eyes were shut for approximately a quarter of a mile. I assumed he'd been too tired at the time to shout or try to wake me up.

I respectfully recommend that you do not try this yourself. Always stay awake when driving, flying planes, cycling, operating heavy machinery, walking down dangerous urban streets and so on.

ERLINDA, MEDICINE WOMAN

Erlinda was a Navajo medicine woman who'd found life on the reservation too stifling and constricting. She'd been drawn to Taos, where she lived among the Anglo community in a very assimilated post-hippie sort of style. To make a living, she gave tarot readings. Obviously, there's no overt connection between the traditional tarot and the Native American way of life (Native American-style pseudo-tarot decks notwithstanding), but she was blessed with finely developed intuition. As any good card reader will tell you, the cards are merely there to trigger the intuition of the reader – not to give any actual messages themselves. Erlinda visited me for acupuncture treatments, and we agreed to swap them for instruction on reading the cards.

She showed me all sorts of spreads, and methods of interpreting their meanings, which ranged from elaborate 12-card layouts all the way down to simply flicking the deck in a certain way, causing the odd card to tumble out and then using it to form the message one needed.

Her focus with me, like Dan's and Govinda's, was to help me develop my intuitive skills. To this end, she'd have me dance about the room like a loon to release my inhibitions, and then I'd shuffle the deck and lay out all 78 cards one by one. As I did so, I'd tell her whatever story was coming into my head. I noticed that when I was with her, basking in the warmth of her ever-watching, smiling face, my intuition would go up a few notches. It took many years of practising on my own before I reached that state solo.

I'd like to tell you a startling story about Erlinda but have none, other than that she helped me become a proficient reader, a skill that continues to serve me well. I tend to use the cards for myself quite frequently in the same way that another person might use a security surveillance system: to afford myself a glimpse of what's occurring behind the scenes of the everyday, of things that might otherwise be blocked from sight – as well as occasionally using the tarot deck, when called upon, to help others in the same way.

RABBI JUDITH

Judith was one of the most spiritually refined people on the planet at that time in 1980, without a doubt. She was a wonderful combination of apparently conflicting aspects somehow all harmonised into a package of absolute serenity and containment, with bright blue eyes and a face like sunshine.

She was a lesbian, a fully fledged rabbi, and an expert in the esoteric Kabbalah system, which has been heavily influenced by New Age thinking and philosophy. This was an unusual combination even then, in light of the mostly male-dominated world of Judaism in which she practised.

I used to be an honorary member of the then-fairly-substantial Taos lesbian sisterhood – only one of two men to be awarded that honour at the time. This was on account of my teaching tai chi to many of the women and becoming good friends with them due to my relatively well-developed feminine side and general love of and respect for womankind. Indeed, had I been a woman, I'd have had a rip-roaring time of it. *They* all certainly were, living in world-renowned architect Michael Reynolds's revolutionary, half-buried, glass and adobe, solar- and wind-powered, fully eco-friendly *Volkshomes* out on the mesa, where they were enjoying an ongoing solar-powered party and exploration into the deeper meaning of existence. And Judith functioned as their spiritual leader.

We bartered our skills: I taught her tai chi, and she taught me Kabbalah, specifically the 'tree of life' aspect of it. I was keen to learn this, as it makes up the backbone of Western esoteric systems. I was then, as now, interested in comparative studies, if only to make progressively more sense of the Taoist system in the way that it relates to all the others.

I found the Kabbalistic meditation style to be hugely powerful, and it certainly added flavour to the Taoist practice: a pleasing metaphysical cocktail for the spiritual hedonist. At one point, I even succeeded in seeing God's face: it was my own but more golden and glowing. I understood that everyone who practises this system enough will experience this phenomenon. Perhaps that's half of the meaning of the notion that God created man in His own image, except in reverse. Or maybe the guys who transcribed the Bible got it backward, and the *his* referred to the man as opposed to the Almighty. Who knows?

Another time, after a few more months of practice,
I even scored a full-on epiphany. I was meditating
in front of Taos Mountain, standing with the tai chi
group behind me about to start the long form together.
Suddenly, unbidden and out of nowhere, I was filled with
a presence. It was a male presence that was so loving,
warm and compassionate that tears started streaming
down my face spontaneously.

As you may remember from my time spent with
Ronnie Laing, I'm not one who's given to gratuitous floods
of tears. So at first, in my most eloquent North London
street language, I told it to fuck off. That's always my
strategy with entities. Tell them to fuck off first and see
what happens. If they do, you know that it was just your
imagination or a flimsy old entity you wouldn't want to
bother with anyway. But if they don't fuck off and are
still there even after repeating the command three times,
they're real and need addressing.

This presence – call it the Christ energy, if you will (it
was Good Friday, as it happens) – was so powerful that it
simply stayed where it was: mostly in my chest. No words
are adequate to describe the love it filled me with. Suffice
it to say, this divine energy transformed me radically from
that day on.

Both of these experiences, framed as they were in the
Judaeo-Christian context, were almost definitely made
available to me through the Kabbalah practice. It's hard
to be 100 per cent sure, though. I was learning and taking

in so much powerful stuff all at the same time in those days that it could have been one or more of a plethora of aspects of training firing off my synapses like that.

However, epiphanies aside, I was still way more drawn to the feeling and simplicity of the Taoist path, so I eventually dropped the Kabbalah training after a year. I'd taken from it enough understanding, colours, and flavour to inform my practice in a helpful way and hopefully, through teaching tai chi to one of its dedicated proponents, contributed to it somehow as well.

MORGAN SHANNON

'It's not your money. It's not your looks. It's not even your dick. It's your clarity they want.' This was Morgan Shannon's pronouncement at our first meeting.

I'd heard about this amazing guy who'd come to town: he was a Reichian therapist, which was an uncommon speciality back then, and still is even today – practitioners are few and far between. Wilhelm Reich's *The Function of the Orgasm* had been on the official unofficial Ronnie Laing reading list, so I was eager to meet a real-life Reichian therapist, and made it my mission to track him down.

I finally spotted him in the old town plaza. Up walked this character with startling blue eyes. His hair was grey on the sides and bald on top, and he was of indeterminable age (mid-40s-ish), possessing more vitality and energy than I'd ever seen in one person before. It was like watching a rocket zooming toward me – not so much in terms of speed, but in the sheer amplitude of personal presence. In fact, to this day, I don't think I've met a more charismatic man.

'Are you Stephen the tai chi teacher?'

'Yes?'

'Morgan Shannon. I hear you've been looking for me.'

'Yes, I have!' I replied excitedly as we shook hands. His handshake was extremely firm, requiring full presence of mind to stop the bones of my hand from caving in.

'I've read *The Function of the Orgasm* and am fascinated by Reich's work,' I said. 'The way he seemed to blend Oriental medicine and philosophy with psychotherapy, and how the *orgone* (vital energy) is the same as *chi* . . . I'd just really love to learn some of it.'

Normally, to approach a therapist of any discipline and ask if he or she will teach you a few bits and pieces of something that's taken a lifetime to learn and develop would be considered cheeky, but as far as I can tell, a bit of cheek every now and then can get you a long way. So I brazened it out. He sat there in silence for a while, and I fully expected him to tell me to get lost.

'Well, I've always wanted to learn some tai chi and they say you're the man, so I'd be up for teaching you. Why do you want to learn it?'

'I'm fascinated by the mind-body connection, and as far as I know, Reich was the first to introduce bodywork into psychotherapy. I studied with R. D. Laing back in England, so I'm quite familiar working with mental states and how they correspond to physical patterns.'

'Are you? How's your sex life?'

I've always enjoyed it when people throw me and can make me blush, whether it's in tai chi or by hurling unexpected apparent non sequiturs my way.

We fell into an in-depth discussion about sex, specifically about women and what makes them tick from a man's point of view – if indeed such generalisations hold any water, which I'm not sure they do. We were talking about what makes women want men, and that's when he gave me the dictum, which has stuck in my mind ever since.

'I mean, look at me,' said Morgan, 'I'm middle-aged and bald. I'm not particularly great-looking, I'm not rich, and my cock's not so huge, but I'm with Rachel, who is only 25 and loves me so much that she'd do anything for me.' At this point, as if on cue, up walked Rachel, who was a real beauty.

He introduced us and smiled with pleasure, appreciating the way she apparently admired *me*, but there was no jealousy, no possessiveness – just pure confidence in himself. I admired him for that. I admired them both: they were a handsome, vibrant couple. Morgan evidently admired me, too, for my natural, easy, honest and candid English way. So lots of admiring was happening. Then it stopped being that, and he got down to business.

He spent a moment looking deeply into my eyes, as if scanning the inside of my skull.

'I'm going to work with you once a week. The first thing I'm going to do is change the way you see things. I'm going to change your vision.'

I understood that the Reichian system involves working through the blockages in five main regions (the ocular, oral, thoracic, abdominal, and pelvic), and the therapist cuts in on the pattern wherever he or she can best find an access point. It's all very similar to the Taoist approach. I was delighted to be starting with the ocular and told him so. 'I love changing my perspective. It's my favourite pastime,' I explained.

And so we began. I taught him and Rachel tai chi, which was a total pleasure, engaging with their relationship via the ancient practice and watching them loving each other through the push hands and so on. I learned a lot about love watching those two, and they learned some neat tai chi manoeuvres.

For my sessions, I'd go to his place every Friday morning.

I loved these sessions, as they truly, radically shifted the way I was seeing – metaphorically *and* literally. It was as if my ocular region were subtly changing shape as years of unconsciously collected tension dissolved.

This invariably set me up for the weekend, when I would take my new toy out to play, looking at as many amazing mountain views as I could (and there were *many* amazing mountain views there).

At that time, as part of the loosening-up process, I got into the dangerous but addictive habit of mountain biking. This entailed two of us driving a pickup truck (with two mountain bikes in the back), miles and miles up steep, deeply rutted dirt roads to the top of one of the smaller, drivable mountains. We'd unload a bike, then one of us would drive the truck back down to the bottom and wait while the other would have the thrill of biking down the mountain. Then we'd switch. If it sounds a bit tame, try riding down the steep slopes of a deeply rutted dirt mountain one day and you'll see what I mean when I say that it's perilous and I'm more than lucky to be here to tell you about it. But the rush is unsurpassed, as far as I'm concerned. In my experience, it leaves skiing, snowboarding, rappelling down rock faces, paragliding, or jumping off 100-foot cliffs into cold rivers behind for sheer thrills.

My point is that before Morgan I wouldn't have risked my neck like that, especially without a helmet. But now, each week my view had been growing broader and deeper, and as it did, my willingness to take risks and live life more fully was growing with it.

Working with Morgan was one of the most exciting openings of the psyche and external-life-reflecting-that-back-at-me processes I've experienced . . . and I've experienced a few. One session particularly sticks in my mind.

Having worked the ocular region extensively, Morgan wanted to make a start on the other regions. He had me lie on my back on the treatment couch, knees up, both arms reaching toward the ceiling, my lips as pouty as I could get them, and saying the word *Mummy!* over and over, while stretching higher with one arm and then the other.

He kept me doing it for what seemed like 20 minutes, until I was totally entranced by the sound and movement. Then suddenly, from the other side of the room, he shouted as loud as can be: 'Don't do that!' which threw me into momentary shock. Immediately, he was upon me, pressing down into my belly, where I'd just tensed from the shock. What he was doing was amplifying my physical holding patterns developed from protecting myself against all the various traumas of growing up, and then releasing them. It was an ingenious device and catapulted my opening process by a quantum leap.

Over the course of a year, Morgan took me through a full 180-degree unwinding process. At the other end of it, he left town without even a word, and no one knew where he went.

He was like an angel who had come down from the sky to sort me out and then vanished as soon as the work was done, although I'm sure there's a more practical explanation. Many years later, I heard that someone had spotted him in the Bay Area but never had it confirmed. His way of working with me, in turn, affected the way I started to work with others. As well as setting me straight (or as straight as someone can be set on what women want), he introduced me to my emotions and the emotional level of others – something that Taoist medicine doesn't reach into as deeply, and I'm forever grateful to him.

MICHAEL REYNOLDS

Michael Reynolds is a revolutionary eco-architect, inventor, polymath, genius and excellent musician. He built an entire solar- and wind-powered eco-village out on the mesa complete with a huge crystal-capped pyramid with an internal meditation chamber. I had some of the most awesomely powerful meditation sessions of my life in it, often finding myself communing spontaneously with ancient Egyptian gods who would appear unbidden in the darkness.

This was back at the turn of the 1980s, and well ahead of its time. His design was so energy efficient that he was selling sizable amounts of energy back to the national grid, and was also able to stage solar- and wind-powered rock concerts.

His own place was the largest *Volkshome* of all, dug into the earth at the rear, and opening out through a huge plate-glass front to the astounding view of the Taos mesa. I used to go there for jam sessions, where sometimes up to 50 musicians would gather, and it was these sessions that inspired me to invest so heavily in my own music. My idea for the 'drum-offs' that I subsequently held in London and New York in 1985 (where I'd get up to a thousand people playing drums together at once) came directly from one night at his place.

It was at a party, where about a hundred people were standing around talking. In the corner, I spotted one of Tell Us Good Morning's tom-tom drums. As I'd run out of talk for the time being, I picked it up and started softly drumming a pattern with my palms, rather than using the mallet. I was looking down at the skin vibrating, absorbed in the rhythm for quite some time. When I looked up, to my surprise, the whole crowd was dancing, and quite wildly too. That was when I realised the simple power of rhythm more acutely than ever before, and it was that which inspired me to start the drum-offs. (They're in abeyance for now, but I suspect that the world hasn't heard the last of them, as they really were phenomenal, and I'll be using elements of them in my Travelling Medicine Show.)

Yet again, I've indulged my occasional tendency to digress, so thank you for bearing with me. The theme of my discussions with Michael was mostly centred on quantum physics and the nature of illusion. One day he called me into his small laboratory-style room in a tower at the top of the house. He'd constructed a mobile that hung in the centre of the room, suspended from the apex of the roof. Around the walls, he'd set up mirrors.

'Look at the mobile,' he instructed. It was perfectly still. As I allowed my gaze to focus on it, it started rotating; and the more I focused, the faster it rotated. 'Now look away and watch what happens in the mirror.' As I turned away to catch the reflection, the mobile slowed down and came to a stop.

I tried it three or four times more, repeating, 'Wow!' over and over.

'The observer affects the field' was all that he had to say in response to my dumbfounded excitement to have witnessed such a display of real-life magic. That's where I got my proof that we each create our own appearances of reality.

Scott MacHardy

Scott MacHardy, seasoned mountain man – with his thick blond thatch of hair, walrus moustache, plaid shirt, jeans, and heavy boots – taught me how to toughen up from my city-boy softness and embrace the more physical aspects of the high-country life.

Shortly after we first became friends, when I'd just arrived in Taos with urban grime still coating my aura, one of his goats had a run-in with a porcupine and was bleeding heavily from the chin. So off we went in his pickup to the local vet, the goat bleeding on my lap.

'I've never even touched a goat before, let alone had one bleed on my trousers,' I remarked. 'There aren't too many around London.' Scott laughed. I was an oddity and curiosity to him. We'd struck up a firm friendship pretty much as soon as I'd arrived in town. He'd come to me to learn tai chi, and we developed an unspoken trade: I'd teach him tai chi, and he'd bring out the mountain man in me. The goat was lesson one. Lesson two followed immediately at the vet's, which consisted of my overhearing the two of them discussing mountain lions as the physician removed the quills from the goat's bleeding mouth. Apparently, the lions had been down around the town rummaging for food in rubbish bins, as the snows had been heavy that winter and the mountains so cold.

'What – real lions?' I suddenly piped up. 'Real lions, here?!'

I simply hadn't accounted for New Mexico being so larger-than-life. Prowling urban foxes, rats, dogs, cats, pigeons and the occasional harmless city spider I was used to, but mountain lions rummaging through high-country garbage cans was simply too way-out of my usual frame of reference: the very notion sent my brain into convulsions.

What was beautiful about Scott (and why we were able to be such close friends across such a huge cultural divide in some senses) was that he was always fascinated by the existential process and so eager to discuss it. I didn't have to act tough or pretend that the notion of mountain lions rummaging through my rubbish was an everyday, nothing-remarkable occurrence for me. I was able to disclose my irrational city-boy fears at every instance. He, in turn, was able to disclose his own concerns, which mostly amounted to fear of what the human race was doing to the planet.

We used to go up into the mountains, where he'd show me how to forage, discerning which plants were edible, medicinal, psychotropic or just plain poisonous. One day, up pretty high, we were trudging endlessly, my backpack getting heavier by the step, when he pointed to a pile of steaming excrement on the ground. 'See that?' he asked, gesturing downward. 'That's bear shit.'

'Wow! *Real* bear shit?' I was fascinated, my gaze riveted to this inert pile of steaming shit on the ground. For me, looking at it was every bit as powerful as seeing the actual bear that dropped it. In fact, the bear would have been an anticlimax – and not, of course, because of any twisted bear-shit fetish on my part. It was the raw, naked reality of a wild animal that big walking along the same path and uninhibitedly taking a dump on it, probably only steps ahead of us.

Scott taught me how to climb big mountains. Walking up a big mountain in the Rockies is quite a feat and takes a fair amount of fortitude and determination. Even the great frequency with which we did it – at every opportunity from May through to November when the snows had melted and the weather was sufficiently mild – still had no effect on lessening the challenge.

We'd occasionally go up to Wheeler Peak, the highest point in the Sangre de Cristo range. From there, on a clear day, one could see out all the way past Los Alamos to Albuquerque, which is 120 miles south. It took hours and hours to get up there and necessitated balancing precariously on razor-thin crests in the manner of a tightrope walker, but the reward of the view from the top was overwhelming. We could actually see the curvature of the earth up there. And the wind howled. In fact, it howled so loudly and furiously at all times that it was impossible to talk; I couldn't even open my mouth. And the sunlight, normally brighter than plausible even down at town altitude, was yet more blinding up here. So a person couldn't stay long – it was simply too much for the senses to bear.

This still serves as a metaphor for me: you spend years working on a project with a peak ahead to scale, and when you finally get there, you can't stay very long to enjoy it because it's simply too much for your senses. So don't give the end result too much importance. The journey getting there is probably far more significant, and making your way down on the other side is most likely where the truly valuable learning can be done.

The other thing that all this mountain walking taught me was perceptual depth, in the sense that when you look at a range of mountains, it resembles a two-dimensional wall of sorts. You develop a visual relationship with that wall effect, as if that's what makes up the whole range. But as soon as you walk up into the mountains, you realise that there is no wall. Instead, a vast three-dimensional universe of rises, dips, peaks and valleys exists, moving off in all directions and set at a variety of unexpected angles that stretch back for miles.

This has always served as a reminder for me not to assume that the surface appearance of something is how it actually is.

It was on such an expedition, while sitting on a rock on the side of Wheeler Peak, looking out at what seemed like the whole planet, that I had the vision, as if from above, which shaped my whole career and life from then on.

I saw a bright, colourful setting with warm, throbbing music supporting the dissemination of ancient Taoist wisdom in an atmosphere of excitement and passion. That's about as succinctly as I can describe it, which doesn't do it justice, as it hit me with a huge impact and has informed my path ever since.

I shared my vision with Scott. He listened and remained silent for a while, considering it. Then he smiled and said 'Wow!' a couple of times. 'Be careful it doesn't kill you.'

For some reason, we both found that amusing. Probably because it was me, the young Taoist, seemingly being so rebelliously at odds with the traditional Taoist approach of keeping your wisdom to yourself, eschewing fame and fortune, and mostly remaining out of the general thrust of human progress. Scott and I fell into a mad fit of the giggles.

Other than introducing me to mountain life, perhaps the most important thing Scott taught me had to do with animals. We live in a world of animals as well as humans; and by watching animals, you get a much clearer picture of what makes humans tick. So don't be fooled by all the airs, graces and other visible effects of human socialisation, for they're only skin-deep.

CHUCK HOLDEN

On the surface of things, Chuck Holden was no spiritual master. He was a handsome devil in his tight jeans, cowboy boots and jauntily cocked Stetson; and he had a keen eye for the ladies. He owned a real-estate company in town, flew a small plane, drank beer almost all day, smoked profusely, watched hefty amounts of porn and laughed a lot. In fact, he was probably the happy-go-luckiest person I've ever met.

His office was opposite Michael's Kitchen, where I used to go for breakfast in the morning. After a few times spotting each other, we introduced ourselves and fell into conversation.

As with most people I met there, I was an oddity to him: a quirky Englishman with long hair and a big smile who taught some exotic Chinese slow-motion boxing that most people hadn't heard of. After talking in-depth through about four cups of coffee, Chuck surmised that I'd forgotten how to enjoy myself, that I was so wrapped up in studying and teaching all this arcane wisdom of the ancient East that I'd lost the art of kicking back and having some 'good ol' fun'.

So we agreed to trade: I'd start teaching him tai chi, which was something totally out of his usual frame of reference, in exchange for him showing me how to enjoy myself. This was really just an excuse – a way of formalising the two of us hanging out. It turned out to be an exceptionally fair trade from which we both benefited. Chuck's message was that you really never know how long you've got, so you must never let anything get you down for too long or you're wasting precious time. The techniques he employed mostly revolved around telling jokes; cutting out bullshit in all its aspects; and of course, being willing and able to laugh from deep in the belly at the drop of a hat, which we would do together endlessly. The strange disparity of interests and backgrounds between us made this one of the more special friendships and brotherhoods of my life.

One day, Chuck, who by then had developed the art of enjoyment to the point of being the global master of happiness, met a beautiful hippie girl named Twinkle,

Sprinkle, or Sparkle – regrettably, I could never remember her name. He fell in love and was happier than he'd ever been, which was happier than most people ever know. He took her up in his plane, flew into an unexpectedly thick cloud, crashed into a mountainside and neither of them was ever seen again.

I still expect him to call me up one day out of the blue because it's impossible for me to believe that someone so full of life and joy could ever leave like that. Meanwhile, the gift of enjoyment was his, and he passed it on to me, for which I shall be ever grateful.

PATRIA C. BARBARY

One day a huge silver 1960s Cadillac drove up, and out stepped this handsome woman in her 60s wearing a cowboy hat, Givenchy silk shirt, tight jeans and the fanciest pair of handmade cowboy boots I'd ever seen. She introduced herself as Patria and said she wanted me to teach her tai chi. We became friends at first glance.

We sat and talked and she told me her life story. She was well versed and practised in Western esoteric arts, having originally been a Christian Scientist and ardent admirer of Mary Baker Eddy, its founder. Additionally, she was a master astrologer and had devised a way of forecasting which stocks and shares to buy based on a company's 'birth' chart. It had netted her a few million bucks over the years. Now she was living all alone in a magnificent adobe palace with a large sweeping staircase, right out in the middle of the mesa. She'd had a few husbands in her time, but was now no longer bothered with 'all that'.

It's hard to define what Patria taught me because she taught me so much magic – pure magic in real life. She also bolstered me whenever I was flagging with my studies and would patiently sit and listen to me waffling on for hours about my confusion over the pulses or other obscure challenges.

One day I was driving her Cadillac for the first time: the Queen Mary, as she called it. She wanted me to be able to borrow it whenever I felt like a bit of archaic mobile luxury, and so was taking me out to show me the ropes. We drove up to a busy T-junction, and she could tell I was getting impatient waiting for a chance to turn left. 'If you wait long enough,' she drawled, 'all the traffic goes by.' At that point, what had been a busy road – with cars whizzing by endlessly – cleared as if by magic, affording me ample time to make my turn.

To this day, when waiting to turn onto a busy road, I hear her voice saying that and the traffic invariably clears within seconds to permit me access. I use it in the metaphorical sense, too. Whenever things feel delayed and I'm in a position of waiting my turn to get someone's attention in business, I hear her say those words, and within days, the door springs open as if by magic.

There's another moment with Patria that always comes back to me whenever I'm getting overly serious or earnest about life. One day we were walking back from the foot of the mountain where I'd been showing her some tai chi postures. I was all serious, talking about the Tao and what have you, when she turned to me and, stopping me in my tracks, said, 'If you think this Tao of yours likes it when you're being all serious like that, you're making a big mistake, young man. Never forget that God has a great sense of humour. Whenever you lose *your* sense of humour, you lose your sense of God.'

*** ***

Chapter Eleven

Back into the Urban Frying Pan

I returned to London from New Mexico in March 1983, all fired up with my mission to heal the world, nowhere to live, and a few dollars in my pocket. I was flying by the seat of my pants as always, perhaps even more so than usual, and went to stay at Jeb and Pete's place in Little Venice.

The day after arriving – and this is an example of how deftly the Tao does last-minute-deliverance-from-trouble moves when you need it to – Mel Balaskas of the Active Birth Movement came by. She was excited to hear about my knowledge of acupuncture and asked if I'd help with a birth she was coaching that evening because her usual acupuncturist, Meredith, was away at the time. So I did –

and I was successful in reducing the woman's pain levels
to nearly zero and triggering a relatively fast and easy
birth.

Mel came by in the morning and made a call to
Yehudi Gordon (the globally eminent obstetrician and
gynaecologist to the stars), during which she happened
to mention me and the fine job I'd just done. Yehudi
currently had a patient in the advanced stages of
pregnancy who'd developed dangerously high blood
pressure and asked if I'd be willing to try to help her, too.

I'd often heard of Dr. Gordon in the early days
(pre-New Mexico) but had never met him. However,
the moment he appeared at the door the following
morning to take me to the hospital with him, it was as
if we'd always been close friends. I don't think I've ever
experienced such an instant friendship connection of
such strength before or since: it was a past-life thing.

YEHUDI GORDON

I successfully treated his patient: got her blood pressure
down to normal in one go, and then pretty much had an
instant practice. Yehudi acquired a small room for me to
work in at the hospital and started it off by sending me
a deluge of pregnant women. One thing led to another,
and I never looked back. For many years, I had one of the
most flourishing acupuncture practices in the UK, and

quite possibly the world. I conducted more than 100,000 treatments between 1983 and 2000, only stopping because my book writing and media work took over. At that point, I realised it was time to share with the world all the knowledge I'd gleaned.

Yehudi's gift was to empower people. Had he not been a doctor, he would have been a guru. He certainly had the looks and temperament for it, with his grey beard and twinkly eyes. He refused to play God with his patients and always threw the responsibility for their health and wellbeing back at *them*. He was one of the first medical doctors in the UK, and the world at large, to substantially combine traditional and holistic approaches. He maintained a crew of alternative-medicine practitioners from all sorts of disciplines, enabling him to direct patients to the best course of treatment for their condition, but always with the emphasis that they take command of their own healing process. That was fairly revolutionary back in those days.

A few months into the start of my practice, he sent me a woman who was recovering from a difficult pregnancy and labour and asked if I could help her regain her balance and get her vitality brimming again. She brought her newborn to our appointment and placed her down in a basket by the side of the futon I used for treatments.

As soon as I'd inserted the pins in the mum, the baby started crying. She'd only just been fed, and the crying was evidently from digestive pains. The mother was embarrassed and uncomfortable, so I assured her that it didn't bother me and asked if I could pick the little one up. I felt into the baby's belly with my fingertips and detected a mass stuck around the descending colon. Holding her against my chest – facing out so that her back was resting against me (and so she could see her mum rather than just the white of my shirt) – I started easing the mass with my fingertips and repeatedly worked my way gently around her abdomen in a clockwise direction, following the colon from start to finish, just as I would have with an adult suffering from an intestinal blockage. (In the way that I'd been trained, people are people, no matter how big or small, old or young – essentially, we're all just babies inside.)

She stopped crying almost at once and gradually fell asleep in my arms with a smile on her face. I placed her down in the basket and slowly pulled my hands away to avoid any sudden change of temperature that might wake her up, then continued treating her mother.

To me, it was a totally ordinary event; however, for the mother, it seemed like a miracle.

The next day, Yehudi called me: 'I hear you performed a miracle on a baby yesterday.'

'No, I just did a bit of massage around her colon, and she fell asleep.'

'Can you teach that stuff to parents?'

'I don't think so. I'd be afraid that I'd make the babies cry, and then everyone would think I was a monster,' I confessed.

'Don't be silly! People aren't that stupid. Let's start a weekly class. You teach, and I'll be there with you.'

It felt like a huge risk. This was the first actual baby-massage class of this type that anyone had ever taught in the UK (as far as I knew), and I was dreading that something would go wrong. But because Yehudi was so bold in taking the risk on my behalf, I reluctantly agreed, and the next week we debuted the class at my house. A few mothers showed up with their newborns. We sat in a circle: the women, the little ones on the floor in front of them, Yehudi and me. I started instructing the mums, timidly at first, then gradually with more confidence – and miracle of miracles, none of the babies cried, nor did anyone call me a monster. I found it relatively easy to adapt the Taoist massage routine to such tiny bodies and teach it to the mums. Word soon spread, and within no time at all, Yehudi and I were holding weekly sessions at the hospital attended by upward of a hundred people – including doctors and midwives who'd come from all parts of the world to have a look. Then, of course, the press picked it up.

My very first TV appearance was with a baby named Porsche. It was on a morning news show, and the directors wanted me to demonstrate the colon massage as an antidote to colic. However, owing to the unfathomable essential lunacy of television, they insisted that we keep her nappy on – lest viewers be offended by the sight of a naked baby – making it all but impossible to actually see what I was doing. I had long hair and a beard and spoke very softly at the time, but inside I do recall thinking rather loudly and rebelliously what a bunch of dingbats TV people were.

So it was Yehudi who indirectly got me started on the whole media adventure. It was he who encouraged me to start writing, too. He insisted that we co-author a small book together to sell to the parents I was teaching in the baby-massage classes. We called it *Massage for Life*, for we believed that a baby who was massaged intelligently in this style (promoting free-flowing *chi* throughout the meridian system) would be set up for life – and I still believe that to be the case. I've been blessed to meet up with some of the babies who benefited from that phase and are now young adults. They're the most confident, physically coordinated people you could ever meet.

Without a doubt, those classes were a modest yet significant contribution to human evolution, and the trend spread quickly. These days, baby massage is taught all over the world. Had I been the mercenary type, I would have stayed with it as my sole gig and become the baby-massage maven, but it simply didn't interest me enough. While totally fascinating in itself, the practice is only one small part of the greater picture, and it's always been that and addressing as much of it as possible that fuels my passion.

Writing the *Massage for Life* book was torturous. It was like being back at school. I had no writing style, no defined voice. It was turgid, but fortunately it worked. People liked it, and we went through quite a few print runs over the years. What it really did was show me that I could write, at least well enough for people to gain some value from it.

Yehudi used to say that I was like a big bird – a large, exotic bird circling high in the sky – and every now and then, I'd swoop down and get involved in the way of the world for a while, then fly off again. I wish it were true. It would save me a lot on flights, and there wouldn't be all that farting around at airports.

Meantime, I was present at hundreds of births in those first few years, so I was no stranger to blood and all sorts of mucky human fluids. By nature, I'm actually quite squeamish and had always found it astonishing that I'd been drawn to acupuncture. The idea of sticking pins in anyone would have made my earlier self go into a mild faint. However, as soon as I started studying the practice, it was as if someone else (perhaps from a previous life) took over, and all traces of those former tendencies vanished.

Then one day I was treating a patient who needed a hysterectomy, and she was also allergic to anaesthetics. It was decided that I'd administer acupuncture anaesthesia to her instead. I'd been taught how to do this but had never actually done it. The lower abdominal area is notoriously difficult to anaesthetise with acupuncture. I explained this to her and Yehudi, but they were both adamant that we give it a go. As this was a rare event back then, Yehudi invited a group of ten medical students to observe.

Suddenly, there I was all scrubbed up with my white cotton hat and face mask in an operating room with a group of students watching my every move. I twiddled the knobs on an electro-acupuncture machine, which sent strong pulses into the specially made right-angled needles I'd inserted into the patient's sacral area and the regular ones I'd inserted in her legs and arms. The intensity of the lights, the earnest gazes of the students and the reality of this woman being wide awake and about to be sliced open, as well as the nervousness I was feeling about it all, combined to make me sweat profusely. So much so, I could hardly see as the perspiration poured from my face. I was dripping onto the floor and doing all that I could not to drip on her.

Yehudi opened her up. She started talking about what she was feeling and as she did so, her intestines moved up and down, making it hard for him to see what he was doing. He asked her to stop, but she was loquacious by nature and couldn't. They argued for a short while, her intestines bobbing up and down, and it was becoming progressively surreal. Eventually, however, she simmered down.

'We're at the level of the spine now. Have a look,' Yehudi stated, and the students peered into her open belly. I could only glance, as I was keen to avoid dripping sweat into her and was fighting a powerful urge to throw up and faint. The whole event was way out of my usual frame of reference, and I guess it had thrown me back to my former pre-acupuncture self. At least, the two were struggling for supremacy within me. Yehudi could see what was going on and remarked, 'Stay focused, Big Bird.'

At one point, he said quietly, 'Here, look at this,' gesturing toward her entire reproductive system now in full view: an aspect of womanhood most people never get to view. 'See that? That's what all the fuss is about, Big Bird.' The sweat continued to roll down my face as my mind grappled with this physical deconstruction of the goddess, of idealised womanhood.

The patient was groaning a bit throughout. Every time she groaned, I'd turn up the juice via the knobs on my machine, which were now dangerously soaked in my sweat. And then, suddenly, thankfully, it was all done and we were standing in the scrub room getting changed.

'Fuck, man, I don't know how you do that. You're fucking amazing!' I gushed. I was just about to launch into reporting on my state of sweat-soaked shock when he caught me with a look that said, Shut up – this isn't about your melodrama, Big Bird! That silent look was probably the most important thing he ever said to me.

That, and something else he said after a rip-roaring drum-off gig at St James's Church in Piccadilly. We had blacked out the stained-glass windows and erected a large stage with a 10K sound rig in front of the altar, decked the roof with a plethora of lights, and invited an audience of 800 with drums. Plus, there was a massive set-up onstage: four huge drum kits, samplers, bass guitar, sax, backing singers – the whole kitchen sink. Together we were creating the loudest noises ever heard in that church (if not the world). At least that's how it sounded.

It was a great triumph, and when I got off the stage, Yehudi came up to me and said, 'I'm really jealous of you, Big Bird.' But he said it with such love and honesty that it showed me it's totally natural and okay to feel envious of someone – in other words, it isn't wrong in itself; only the denial of it and consequent acting out unconsciously to punish the object of your jealousy is wrong or destructive.

As well as essentially giving me a successful acupuncture practice and writing and media career, Yehudi also introduced me to easily the most startling and on-the-edge teacher of all, the one who rounded off my training: Frank Kramer. But more on him shortly.

My gratitude to Yehudi is eternal. I'm certain we've been brothers in previous lifetimes as well as this, and will be brothers in many lifetimes to come. And I know there are many who feel the same appreciation in respect to the incredible transformations he facilitated in parents going through pregnancy, birth and the early stages of parenthood. If the entire world possessed his kindness, integrity, and wisdom, we'd be living in paradise.

I owe Yehudi Gordon a great deal. In fact, I still owe him ten grand he lent me a few decades ago (I just remembered that while sitting here typing), so I hope this book sells in sufficient quantities to pay him back. Beyond that, I owe him immense gratitude and respect.

BOB COLEMAN

It was also through Yehudi that I met Bob Coleman, who is the living embodiment of Taoism and without a doubt one of the most powerful tai chi practitioners and teachers in the world. I say this unreservedly, having encountered a fair smattering of extremely influential martial artists and tai chi players, in particular. Although his tai chi is perhaps the least flashy or flowery to look at, and he may be perhaps the least lyrical to listen to of all the great masters, I've never encountered anyone with a better grasp of the actual mechanics of *chi*.

People talk a lot of drivel about this vital energy as if it's something that can only be engaged with mystically. Bob showed me that *chi* is merely a natural product of positioning your body correctly as you move. He had an ability to make even the most esoteric aspects of tai chi feel completely ordinary. The ability to see everything (including the most extraordinary spectacle) as part of the natural order of things, and hence ordinary, is a prerequisite for an enlightened mind. The more you go around thinking that everything's extraordinary or weird, the more you're missing the point. Everything is ordinary, even the Tao. And when you know this, everything instantly becomes extraordinary.

In any case, Bob Coleman was and is extraordinary. He could toss me several feet through the air with the slightest nudge, always laughing heartily when he did so. I studied tai chi, Hsing I, and pa kua with him. He reckoned he was teaching me to do it all properly, as he felt the training I'd received in America was a bit Hollywood and overblown. Bob brought it all back down to the nuts and bolts of how to move the *chi*, and in his prosaic northern English style (which merely hid a wealth of poetic sensibility), he guided me to a sort of completion of the training, although one can never really reach an end point to developing the Taoist arts. To the contrary, you grow by a series of quantum leaps in the practice the more you go along.

Bob expressed stillness in movement – the ultimate aim of Taoist practice and particularly the Taoist martial arts. All parts of the universe are in perpetual motion, including each of us. To reach stillness at the core in the midst of movement is to reach the Tao itself. If I represent the noisier end of the scale concerning the Taoist way, he represents the quiet zone.

A classic example of the Taoist idea of making no waves, Bob eschews attention, acclaim, fame, fortune, ambition and all the racket and clamour of a world chasing its own tail. And even though he's undoubtedly at the very top of his field in terms of ability, talent, and skill, he lives a humble life and is one of the most contented people on the planet. When we first met, we sat down after the lesson one day and fell into discussing the Taoist sperm-retention technique, which builds one's personal power. I'd been practising it for a while and was extolling its virtues.

He agreed. 'It's a very powerful technique, yes . . . but . . . ,' and he turned to me with a playful smile, making the traditional obscene sexual gesture, 'there's nothing like a damn good fuck sometimes!'

Bob taught me, or rather exponentially furthered my learning, to be myself; and I bless him every day as I start my morning's tai chi practice, along with Al Huang, Grandmaster Chi/Flash and the others.

Dan Fauci

I only spent a short time with Dan Fauci, the guy who founded the Actors Institute in New York. He created a workshop course known as the Mastery, which was a derivative of est (Erhard Seminars Training, which promoted personal transformation and empowerment) and provided an incredibly powerful existential shunt for anyone needing to learn how to perform.

I participated in a weekend Mastery course, and it totally blew me apart. I went from being a self-conscious, shy, awkward non-performer (who, other than when teaching tai chi or baby massage, was scared of the sound of his own voice) to a confident, outgoing show-off in 72 hours. And it was all due to Dan.

Dan had the knack of getting people to loosen up and get off their complexes. As participants performed onstage in front of the rest of the class, he would simply stand at the side as they did their piece and direct them to do it as Charlie Chaplin, Shirley Temple, Diana Ross, Winston Churchill, Jack Nicholson and so on. He somehow had a way of looking past people's personality distortions directly into their souls within. I'd sit there in the audience watching folks transform before my very eyes, or I'd be the one onstage experiencing my transformation. It was the most remarkable sensation of sudden release into a new dimension.

I can't really say how his magic worked, other than noticing how in-his-body and confident Dan was. But by the end of that session, I was singing, dancing and all ready to bring my circus to the world.

I wasn't doing it to be narcissistic or because I had any latent desire to show off. I was simply aware that I had to brush up on my performance skills, as I was driven – and still am – to bring everything I teach to the widest audience possible for the sake of making a valuable contribution to the world. Whichever way you cut that, it boils down to performing at some level.

If left to my own devices, I'd sit on a mountainside and do nothing, never speak to anyone, never write a word and never record or perform a single note of music. I would just sit there. But as fate would have it, I'm driven by this perpetual force within that requires total dedication to the mission. It's a paradox, but accommodating it with ease constitutes the greatest wisdom, and I work at it constantly.

So my eternal thanks goes to Dan for drawing me out of myself, for ushering me into the world of performance with such dexterity and aplomb.

JIM THE CLOWN

To build pace I needed to shed more layers of self-limiting inhibition, so I jumped at the opportunity to study with Jim the Clown. We had employed him to stand behind a large latex circular screen hung perpendicular to the floor at the rear of the stage during the drum-off gigs. UV lights were shone onto the screen, and Jim's job was to press his face and hands into the latex, moving around in a bizarre dance. The visual effects this created for the audience were stunning. Anytime I happened to turn around from the front of the stage and check him out, I'd start cracking up, so I had to stop taking peeks at him. However, afterwards, I asked if he'd be up for teaching me how to be a clown like that. He obliged and agreed to come around once a week and train me to be a fool. It was a relatively easy task.

One of his exercises involved him sitting cross-legged high on top of a large chest of drawers in the corner of the room (like the Joker) and me walking, or rather moving, around the room in a circle attempting to act funny. That's all I had to do: be funny. I wasn't allowed to say anything. It all had to be conveyed by body language, facial expressions, and movement. Whenever I wasn't being funny, in his opinion, he'd let out a whistle in the manner of someone summoning a dog.

I don't know if you've ever tried to be funny without speaking, or if you've ever attempted humour in general. If you have, I'm sure you've found that the harder you try, the less funny you become. It was evident amid an almost endless trail of whistles as I circled the room that it was about letting go into being funny rather than trying to be funny. It's a subtle difference and not one you get with the rational mind. Letting go usually necessitates a letting-go of the rational mind.

After a few sessions, there was no more whistling from Jim, and it seemed a natural place to end our meetings.

That was one of the toughest bits of training I ever went through, and it took someone of immense compassion as well as clowning mastery to facilitate it. I'm also grateful for how it spurred me to attempt challenges that I would have never tried otherwise, like running onto a crowded train carriage, singing and playing the guitar for all I was worth and then moving to the next carriage at the next stop, and so on, until I'd 'done' a whole train (with an accomplice in tow passing the hat). I would do these stunts mostly for the adrenaline, but the excuse was that it was my training to help me shed my inhibitions.

I've actually inspired a younger generation of existential explorers who have taken this to a new level: my friend Spencer Mac, for example (in the spirit of losing his pride, as he calls it), walked around the entire ground floor of Selfridges department store in London's hugely busy Oxford Street on the Saturday before Christmas. That's when the store is at its busiest; and the ground floor (where all the make-up, skin-care products, perfume, handbags and costume jewellery are sold) is crammed to the rafters with attractive women, in front of whom a man would prefer not to make a fool of himself. Well, there's nothing so spectacular about Spencer walking around there, you might think, except that he did so while wearing a woman's long auburn-coloured wig complete with a velvet headband.

He said round one made him want to be swallowed up by the floor. By round two, he got over himself; and during round three, he was in his element, chatting freely with every woman on his path. As he was congratulating himself for having just lost such a large chunk of pride, an old man walked slowly past him on the way out of the store. With a completely deadpan expression, he was wearing a pair of oversized false ears. Evidently the master.

Where will the clowning stop?

HUGH MASEKELA

Hugh Masekela is one of the world's greatest trumpeters and one of its most charming and kindly characters. I used to give him acupuncture treatments whenever he was in town for a while. I'd watched him record at the studio and had seen him perform onstage, and was blown away by his playing. It would send me into paroxysms of musical bliss.

One day we fell into talking about life strategies. He'd been up, down, and up again, so he knew the roller coaster well. Hugh told me that I was going to be incredibly famous one day, saying that he could see such things. He told me it would be fun: the limousines, the parties and all the usual clichéd stuff of fame and fortune. He advised me to meet a woman before it happened and hang on to her, because after it all started, I'd never be able to tell if a woman wanted me or my status. It was a quaint piece of advice, but didn't work out in that manner as it happens, although that's by the way.

Hugh asked me if I could have anything in the whole world right now, what would it be? I took a breath and said, 'For you to bring your horn down here next time and play for me.'

So he did.

The next week, he walked in with his trumpet case, took out his instrument, stood in silence with his eyes closed for a moment and then proceeded to blow the most astonishing solo I've ever heard. And it went on and on. And just when I thought I couldn't stand any more, he'd take it even higher.

What Hugh taught me was that no matter how good life gets, it can always get better. His solo remains one of the highlights of my peak experiences.

DR. AKOSH TATAR

Akosh was born in Budapest. He was refinement and finesse personified. A beautiful-looking man with elegant hands, he ran a busy medical practice in Kreuzberg, one of the funkier parts of Berlin. The wall was still up in those days, and the city had a fantastic siege mentality and pressure-cooker effect in terms of synergy among people.

As well as being a general practitioner, Akosh had trained in acupuncture, homeopathy, and hypnotherapy. He developed a system of prescribing allopathic medicines specifically for the side effects they'd produce and then work on the latter using a combination of holistic therapies. He believed that integration was the key to achieving the best results in actually healing his patients rather than merely masking the symptoms. His clientele were avant-garde, and the atmosphere at his practice was a bit like a Zen monastery on acid, with a large gold Buddha, incense, and nihilist techno or space dub playing on the sound system. (He was also the inventor of one of the most amazing psychotropics ever devised: it was a combination of ketamine and dopamine that sent you off on a trip that lasted hours and made you feel like you were composed of marshmallows.)

Akosh was interested in investigating telepathy with me. So during one session, Frank, Akosh, my French friend Gerard and I were sitting in a circle on the floor. (Akosh spoke Hungarian, German and English. Frank spoke English and German, and Gerard spoke only French. I spoke English, German and French.) We proceeded to have a four-way conversation of great depth about the nature of reality and how it oscillates between existence and non-existence so rapidly that we can't detect it, in precisely the way computers work with their ones and zeros.

Akosh was speaking in German, Frank in English, Gerard in French; and I was mostly listening in all three. And although none of us were trilingual enough to understand everything that everyone said, we completely understood each other as if the meaning of the words was being conveyed in sound molecules rather than word and sentence construction. It was utterly astonishing.

Once the trip wore off, no one could really understand anyone again, and the world returned to normal . . . or the illusion of it.

Akosh and I also used to discuss the issue of life after death in depth. During another session, it was clear to both of us that what we think of as death is merely an illusion, and that who we are is far larger than can be confined in a single body or expressed in a single personality. What we are is endless and goes on forever. This was clear. However, upon touching down again on solid ground, it was hard to recall that clarity.

'What troubles me is that we have brains, and everything we've just experienced took place by virtue of those brains,' I said. 'When we die and no longer have brains, where will we be able to experience anything?'

He smiled with all the wisdom in the universe and said in his most refined Hungarian accent, 'I don't fucking know!'

We both laughed. His big message was to cease to draw conclusions if you wished to arrive at conclusions of any worthwhile kind.

One day I met with a patient who had suffered some sort of awful trauma in childhood but couldn't recall what had happened. She reckoned that she had blotted it from memory. Still, she was suffering so much inordinate stress that she believed had resulted from this unspecified event, and it was making her life miserable. We agreed that during the next acupuncture session, I'd also do a regression and take her back to the trauma so that she could dispel it from her system both mentally and energetically.

I took her gradually back from adulthood to three years old, whereupon she started convulsing so hard that the treatment couch was violently jumping about. I tried every trick from a vast toolkit to bring her out, but nothing was working. Removing the pins and keeping one hand on her (lest she fell off the couch altogether), I called Akosh in Berlin, interrupting him with a patient, and quickly explained the situation. Without hesitation, he told me to whisper in her ear three times, saying, 'You are alive.'

'What? You reckon it's that simple?' I asked incredulously.

'Do it!' he commanded more than suggested.

So with him still on the line, I leaned over the woman and whispered, 'You are alive!' three times. Lo and behold, she stopped convulsing instantly, and from that moment on – and as long as we remained in contact, at least – she enjoyed a new, unprecedented level of relaxation and inner peace.

Akosh taught me to reduce things to the nub, to reduce complexity to simplicity and to desist from seeking to draw conclusions but to allow them to draw themselves.

JÜRGEN KOLB

Jürgen looked like a large, scary skinhead. He had no time for sentimentality and had the ability to see right through someone's act to what was really going on inside, and then he'd address it rather than deal with the façade. He was a skilled hypnotherapist and practised master of aspects of NLP (neuro-linguistic programming). We used to play a game consisting of him dropping me into a trance and bringing me back out again from moment to moment in the midst of normal conversation. He did it so adroitly that I found myself giggling foolishly most of the time I spent around him.

Because he was so unsentimental and had such a wry sense of humour, he invited brutal honesty. Consequently, I was able to voice any untoward feelings I had about him without first editing them. There aren't many people who are so self-possessed that you can insult them all day without them feeling a bit miffed, but Jürgen seemed to actively relish this.

Although he looked scary, Jürgen was really an angel in disguise. He had started his working life as an emergency medic and had seen the dark underbelly of life close-up. This had given him a striking level of compassion, which, when combined with his tough exterior, made him a great target for making fun of; and I'd do it mercilessly. Somehow, in this strange trade-off, it seemed only proper that he teach me the tricks of his trade, with which I could be of more help to my patients.

Specifically, these tricks entailed using combinations and variations of vocal patterns such as speech tempo, rhythm, tone and cadence to map out different levels of conversation. Everything you say directly to a person's unconscious – the place where we actually make our choices – will be detected by the unconscious as being specifically aimed at it. And the premise is that the subconscious only recognises the positive aspect of any statement. So if you tell someone not to smoke, the only word that his or her subconscious picks up is *Smoke!* On the other hand, if you say 'I wouldn't want you to . . .' then pause subtly, deepen your tone and decelerate your tempo, continuing with: 'do something different now,' you can be sure the person will subsequently do something different, regardless of you saying the opposite.

Polarity responding (this tendency people have to respond in a way contrary to the overt command) is used as part of the technique. So for instance, when you know an individual will rebel against any positive suggestion you give, tell him authoritatively: 'Don't . . . feel good now.' And he'll start feeling good in spite of himself.

I've found it useful when treating people for addiction (especially heroin), and when helping someone find the inner strength and courage to confront a life-threatening disease. But mostly I just loved learning about the unconscious mind. I've always believed that it's the subconscious mind that holds the key to human evolution, both individually and collectively.

During this period, I was also working with a friend on a project. She was an artist and indulged fully in the artistic temperament. She would burst into tears at the drop of a hat, and if I didn't watch it, I'd spend most of the day attempting to keep her chirpy, so we'd avoid the distraction and delay caused by her interminable blubbering.

She was a militant feminist too, which seemed to encompass broaching no suggestions that she pull herself together. If she wanted to cry all day, it was her right as a woman to do so, she once told me emphatically.

One day – for the sake of experiment and with her consent – I invited Jürgen down to the studio where we were working. He didn't say much in general, and other than the initial handshake, the two of them didn't say a word to each other.

During the course of the morning, there were only three crying interludes, and they hadn't lasted long. We were making great progress, until something caught my friend's eye outside the window that triggered her, and she went off into a full-blown sobbing session. Although I had forewarned Jürgen about her militant feminism, he walked slowly over to her, stood behind her, and simply said: 'Oh, do stop that, you snivelling bitch!'

Upon hearing this, she spun around to face him, and I assumed that Jürgen was about to receive a hefty slap across the face or punch in the jaw. But instead she started to laugh. She laughed and laughed. From deep in her belly, she laughed as if she'd never laughed before, and it went on and on. And you know, I've never seen her cry since.

*** ***

Chapter Twelve

Being Frank

I've been saving Frank Kramer for last. This is partly because he was the last real teacher I had and the one who put all the finishing touches on me before I became The Barefoot Doctor, and partly because my story and education with him were the most startling of all. My experience with Frank was totally unprecedented and took me to places I never dreamed existed. He made everything I had studied up to that point come fully to life.

One day Yehudi came bounding into the hospital. The day before he'd been a guest speaker at a large Buddhist gathering and was all fired up from it. He'd been invited to lecture on the subject of birth, a topic on which he was an undisputed master. And the guest speaker who had been invited to talk about death was a breath therapist named Frank.

'You've got to meet this guy. He's very interesting and knows quite a bit about death. He can teach you a lot.'

I agreed, and he invited Frank along to the next baby-massage session.

That morning I was walking around doing my usual greeting with all the parents and saying hello to the babies (and getting a handle on which of them would be most likely to erupt into tears at any moment so I could be ready to dart in their direction and do the silencing magic, if required). Then in walked one of the strangest-looking characters I'd ever seen. I remember thinking, Fuck me. He's weird – that must be Frank.

Bear in mind that this was 1983: way before shaved heads and straight men wearing women's clothes were in any way fashionable. Here he was with his shiny bald dome, strange Elton John-like spectacles, a V-neck cashmere sweater (with a discreet diamond brooch), leggings, Birkenstock sandals, and toenails painted black. He was standing by the door with his two-year-old son and the nanny.

I went up to him at once. 'Are you Frank?'

'Yes. Are you Stephen?' he asked in a slightly theatrical tone.

I thought to myself, Wow, this is the weirdest guy I've ever met. I must be friends with him!

'Yes, I am he,' I replied, mimicking the theatrics. He laughed. I laughed. And that was it: we were friends. It was exactly the same as it had been with Yehudi, except he was the angel of light who brought people into the planet, and Frank was the dark angel who was all about people leaving the planet. And both were Geminis. It seems rather odd now, yet at the time, it felt like the most natural thing in the world to arrange to trade sessions with Frank right there on the spot: I'd give him acupuncture, and he'd do breath therapy with me.

He came to me for the first session. One of my techniques involved intelligently pushing deep into the abdomen – specifically into the liver, solar plexus, and spleen regions – where all the emotions get stuck, pushing until a release happened on the physical plane, which would then translate into a release on the psycho-emotional plane. Most people could only take so much pressure, as it's quite a sensitive area. Frank, however, just wanted more and more until my whole body weight was behind the push, at which he made the strangest high-pitched sounds like a wounded wolf.

'Do you want me to stop?'

'No, push more!'

He had studied at Esalen in Big Sur, California, with the pioneer of breath therapy, Stanislav Grof. Breath therapy also encompassed LSD therapy, MDMA therapy and ketamine therapy, I discovered as time went by.

During the first session Frank gave me, he turned on some fast-moving pre-trance music, specifically produced for this sort of work. He asked me to lie down on the treatment couch and breathe quite rapidly, more or less taking in twice as much air as I was exhaling. He kept a hand on my diaphragm area most of the time, and if my breaths wavered, he'd say, 'Breathe!' His voice was the most sonorous of any I've ever heard, even more so than Orson Welles. Frank was actually known around town as 'The Voice'.

'Breathe, just breathe!' He was also succinct with his words, never wasting a single one, as if each was worth a million bucks. But he said, 'Breathe, just breathe!' so often over the years that it became his mantra.

After a few minutes of this, I felt high in a way that's similar to when you're given laughing gas at the dentist's surgery. The sensation afforded me a fairly instant experience of the divinity within and all around, and I loved every minute of it. Afterwards, as I was saying 'Wow!' a lot and being rather gushy, he asked me about my Taoist meditation practice. I explained the micro- and macrocosmic orbits: shooting the *chi* around various meridians in the body to develop awareness of the immortal spirit-body; and so on, as well as to attain longevity.

'Are you one of the longevity brigade, then?' he asked.

'Yes, of course, why would I be anything else?'

'Oh, I'm one of the short-and-sweet brigade.'

'Really? What do you mean?'

'I'm bored, and at some point, I'm going to take my own life.'

'Bored?! How can you be bored?' I asked incredulously. I couldn't see how anyone so evidently enlightened could possibly feel that way.

'I'm bored,' he repeated. 'Utterly existentially bored.'

'Wow.' I didn't know what else to say. 'I'll show you stuff that will stop you from feeling bored. Do you know tai chi?'

'Yes, I've been doing tai chi for years.'

We pushed hands, and although he was a diminutive character, he was clearly able to gain the advantage on me without strain. 'I'll find things to reinspire you,' I promised. I was strongly drawn to him and could see he was a genius. And there began a 12-year game of me finding things to hold his interest in life.

In exchange, I had the most fun and one of the most educative rides imaginable. It would be hard to conjure up more entertainment than what occurred in those 12 years, during which we became the closest of friends.

Frank was a master of words, and I'd often pester him to write a book. His ideas were totally original and right on the mark, but he'd always just say, 'There are already too many words in the world without me adding to them.' Interestingly, it was he who taught me how to write – that is, he taught me adult English. At first I applied it to songwriting and gradually progressed to books. But it was Frank who got my mind around the notion of grabbing chunks of internal dialogue and transcribing them onto pages.

He could always be relied upon to come up with an oblique angle on any topic, and his answers to questions were like keys that unlocked doors that had been jammed shut forever. I don't know if I can stick to any logical, sequential, or chronological order in telling a story; and in any case, consistency was anathema to Frank. Indeed, none of the assumed middle-class niceties we all hold in such great store meant anything to him. He wouldn't buy anyone birthday gifts or Christmas presents – not even his own son – simply because he couldn't see why he should. However, he was quite capable of suddenly buying someone a house. He had this magic knack of making money in the oddest ways and always had a great surfeit. He used money as a way to spark up 'theatre', often offering loans to people for the strangest projects and not expecting to get a penny back. He just wanted to see what would happen.

He never bowed to convention, yet he was so self-assured, so self-possessed, that no one ever took offence.

One night we went out to visit a friend, and during the drive we stopped for some kebabs. On that particular evening, as well as his leggings and painted toenails, Frank had chosen to don a woman's cheap-looking, platinum-blonde wig, on top of which he was wearing a Rasta-style knitted hat. As we pulled up to the kebab shop, the entire New Zealand rugby team, who were in town for a game, decided to walk in just ahead of us.

Oh, no, I thought, with all my middle-class values coming to the fore, I don't want to witness this. I imagined that they'd attack him for being some kind of freak. I waited outside for a moment to gather myself, preparing to use my martial-arts skills to rescue him. But when I walked in, there he was in the middle of the group, and they were dancing the conga and laughing like lunatics. They loved him. He was their instant hero, their leader. How the hell did he do that? It was his utter self-belief and knowledge. He created his own reality, and others would go along with it simply because his belief was so strong – at least that's my explanation.

Frank was informally, but indisputably, a guru, and had a relatively large following around him: various friends and dependents, disciples and helpers. He was like a Mafia don or the general of a great secret army. People would do anything for him, no matter how weird or unexpected. He wasn't obviously handsome in any way, yet women would melt around him. And guys did, too – which is how we wound up spending most of that evening with the New Zealand rugby team.

PSYCHEDELIC INVESTIGATIONS

After a while, Frank's breathing sessions developed into LSD sessions.

At one of these, he managed to keep me under control for a few hours just lying there breathing, rather than indulging in mental gymnastics, which was no mean feat. During this, I experienced a major revelation: I had a vision of a Christlike figure with horns and hooves. It disturbed me greatly.

'That's Abraxas,' Frank explained. 'It's time to explore the dark side: God isn't just light, you know.'

'What do you mean?'

'Well, you always wear white, don't you?' In those days I did; it just appealed to my sense of aesthetics at the time.

'Yeah. So?'

'You're evidently in denial of your dark side.' Until that point, I hadn't even consciously realised that I had one. And so I began the exploration into darkness, required for all seekers and holy people at some point in their journey. It's all well and good promoting the light, but one can't do so authentically without first being versed in, and thus unafraid of, the dark.

We went on to discuss illusions and how we create reality according to our beliefs.

'Would you like to taste something amazing, something unlike anything you've ever tasted before?' he asked enticingly. I nodded. 'Wait here and close your eyes.' He went off into the kitchen for an indeterminable time and came back with something on the end of his finger.

'Here, open your mouth.' I did as I was told, and he pushed in some soft, mousse-like substance that did indeed taste unlike anything I'd ever tasted. It wasn't sweet and it wasn't savoury. It was creamy without being too creamy. It was altogether the most exotic taste sensation I'd ever experienced.

'Wow, what was that?'

He wouldn't answer.

The next day he asked, 'Would you like to know what it was you tasted?'

'Yes!' I replied eagerly.

At which point he produced a tub of Philadelphia Cream Cheese.

'But, but . . .'

But he'd already left the room. He did that easily and frequently.

Frank simply couldn't be bothered to hang around if he was bored, and he would grow bored whenever I wasn't being fully present. This might happen in the middle of a sentence just as I was about to tell him whatever important bit I had been leading up to. He'd simply get up and walk out.

Gradually, LSD sessions gave way to MDMA (Ecstasy) sessions. I have to point out here (lest you mistakenly believe that this is about to turn into a drug-propaganda piece) that back in the early 1980s hallucinogens were used in a relatively responsible fashion by the global-therapy fraternity based in London, Berlin, New York and, of course, California. It wasn't just a big jerk-off, using recreational drugs for fun – although it was mostly highly enjoyable.

Having had the privilege of investigating the effects of hallucinogens in depth over a fairly sustained period in the 1980s and 1990s, and having gained much benefit from it, it might sound hypocritical for me to then say that the time and space no longer seems appropriate for their use. I believe the effects are more likely to be deleterious than beneficial. I also believe that these substances come to us by divine fiat and not by accident, as a form of collective medicine to open up the chakras or psychic centres in the body-mind complex, individually and collectively. When the process is complete, when society at large has got the message, however unconsciously, the sustained use of those substances becomes inappropriate. And in any case, as far as I can tell, these days most of the drugs I see taken are used as an anaesthetic to kill existential pain and anguish rather than to expand consciousness.

However, back then substances used in therapy circles were treated as a high-tech sacrament rather than a cheap thrill, and relatively strict discipline was observed. In the early 1980s, MDMA, for instance, was still legal (or at least not yet illegal). They were calling it ADAM at the time, and you were required to read the literature that came with it, which advised fasting for at least 12 hours before taking the capsule (or capsules, depending on your body weight). During the session, you were encouraged to remain lying down, covered with sufficient blankets to retain body heat; and play soft, emotion-stirring music.

Fauré's Requiem, for example, would be played while the therapist kept a hand on your chest or solar plexus the entire time, reminding you to keep breathing, especially when your eyes started moving rapidly or your jaw started to 'gurn' (churn), indicating that you were getting lost in ego delusions in the forebrain.

The effect was a notable relaxation of the chest and feeling of great warmth as universal love flooded you, along with a sure knowing that God, the Tao – or whatever creates all this – really does love you, hasn't forgotten or forsaken you, and that all was well. So well, in fact, that coming down the other side of that high of wellbeing was a rather steep descent, culminating a couple of days later in a severe case of the blues. And it was this that the therapist made use of to spur you on to the next stage of personal growth. You would have a straightforward talking session on the day of the blues, and what came up would be used to guide your explorations through the next phase of self-discovery.

At the time it was hard to see how MDMA could ever become a street drug. No one had expected that by 1988 its use would be widespread on the dance floor amid the pumping noise and heat. And as for ketamine, I still find myself incredulous that people actually enjoy stumbling about in public on it.

I remember the session when Frank gave me ketamine. When I came out of the trip, the first thing I said was,

'That will never become a street drug. It simply couldn't –
it's just too powerful.'

'Oh, yes it will,' he responded.

Frank was a great seer. He could see clearly into the
future, and I never knew him to be wrong. However, you
couldn't force clairvoyance out of him. You couldn't force
anything out of him, in fact. And he was certainly right
about ketamine. It's a huge street drug now.

I don't think people realise how profound the effects
of this drug are and how profoundly dangerous it can
be. Aside from being a strong anaesthetic that can quite
easily stop your heart, it draws you into the death state –
or eternal-life state, depending on your view – which is
highly seductive. I believe this can easily lead to lowering
your vibrational field enough to indirectly invite untimely
death. The psychological effects are so radically unsettling
that without proper supervision and spiritual, or at least
psychological, preparation, its use can create deeply
disturbing results and cause all sorts of psychoses.

On the other hand, it undoubtedly transports you to
the realm of the gods, wheren with the right focus, you're
able to manifest actual shifts in reality, which in turn shifts
the collective unconscious. But if you multiply the effects
of that by the huge numbers of spiritually unschooled
people using ketamine around the planet on a regular
basis, you'd be forgiven for wondering whether that
usage might be contributing to the ever-increasing tone
of Through-the-Looking-Glass unhinged loss of values

endemic in the world just now. It's also highly physically addictive.

And although I personally sustained great lasting value from that era of experimentation, I'd never go near it or anything like it these days and truly don't want to come across as glorifying this or any other substance. If anything is to be glorified, it's the Tao that is informing our unfathomable intelligence to, among other things, create such remarkable substances rather than the substances themselves.

My interest was and is about achieving the spiritual, transcendent experience. And my desire is to maintain that state in the midst of the everyday world so I never forget my divine nature. My wish is for all of us to walk in the realm of the gods as we work, rest and play, in order to gain full value from each and every moment at the very deepest level – rather than be enslaved by the collective trance of the humdrum.

And at that time, in that context, ketamine was an appropriate path, or sub-path, for me. I can't speak for anyone else. It's all down to personal preference. I've seen what it can show me; I don't need to see it again. I'm living it. Informed by my Taoist training and vice versa, the knowledge received is now integrated into my cosmological blueprint, but I couldn't recommend it as a viable path. On the contrary, I'd recommend avoiding ketamine and any other chemical enhancer. It was relevant to me then, however, and certainly brought to life everything I had studied hitherto in a way I doubt any other substance could have.

However, that was mostly on account of it being integrally connected to Frank and what he was teaching me. The first time I took ketamine was in 1985. I lay down with Frank sitting across the room while another friend, who happened to be a nurse, deftly injected me with just the right quantity (according to my weight) in the muscles of my right buttock. The traditional way was to take some MDMA first to warm you up and reduce your fear levels, without which the ketamine experience tended to be cold and scary. So by the time the injection came, I had no fear. Everything was as it was meant to be.

I lay there with my eyes closed, and all of a sudden it was as if a dozen helicopters, attached to the base of my skull, were lifting me up into an invisible sky. They whisked me up through a multitude of dimensions until I was face-to-face with the divine presence amid an endless field of intricate geometric patterns, presumably the subatomic structure of existence. The presence informed me that great change was coming to the world. It showed me how, in spite of the burgeoning prosperity and apparently endless abundance in the Western world, essential resources were actually being depleted at an unsustainable rate, and that with the rapidly growing population, this would soon cause an unprecedented crisis.

I was viewing a realm in which the linear concept of time no longer held sway and was thus able to tune in

to the same consciousness as, say, the Hopi had many
thousands of years ago, when they made their uncannily
prescient prophecies about our current epoch. It warned
me not to grow too attached to my current perceptual
version of the world, all rosy and secure, and instead to
prepare for a paradigm change so radical that very few
would be able to retain a grip on sanity. The presence
reaffirmed that my role would be to help soften this effect.
It then directed my attention to Frank and bade me to
enter his spine through the coccyx.

I was delighted to discover that my spirit was able
to move freely wherever it wished in the world of
appearances, and I found myself inside Frank's spine.
Halfway along the spinal cord, approximately at kidney
level, I detected a break in the flow of energy. It was
clearly visible as white light with a gap in the stream.
I instinctively set about mending the break by knitting
together the two 'broken ends', as if twisting two ends of
wire to bind them.

Once that was done, I came out and tried
experimenting by tuning in to other people I knew and
entering their bodies to heal them. But I soon grew tired
of that game.

I relaxed back into the greater picture, which was of
one being – the divine presence, informing everything
we know and love on the material plane, as if the world
is merely the cloak of the divine. The presence then bade
me to let go of even that, so there was no observer and

no observed, simply the one being. I was the one being, but because I was merely illusory, there was just the one being pretending it was me, pretending it was you, pretending it was all of us. And it was doing so because as the one being, without pretending you have someone to play with, eternity gets pretty boring and lonely. And then it started forming a sentence. It took a while to come through in sound, and when it did, it was: 'I am love.' Because I wasn't there, now being merely the divine presence's imaginary friend, the illusion of me had to expend a notable measure of energy to hang on to this sentence so that I could bring it back as a treasure from the other side.

Interestingly, as the drug started wearing off (and my local self began subtly re-forming by creating an illusory divide between me and the presence), the sentence transformed itself in my mind into the third person, and I found myself re-entering the everyday state repeating 'God is love,' over and over, as if it were the most original, profound, and radical statement ever. And it is. But unless you're in a transcendent state, through whatever means, where you're actually seeing it yourself, it's merely a pretty-sounding phrase that looks as if it could mean something big, but you're not quite sure what. Eventually, I remembered the essence of it and realised that the phrase should read: Love is God.

In any case, just as fast as the helicopters had lifted me up through the sky of my mind, they dropped me back down. But just before they did, I glimpsed a view of the everyday realm from the transcendent state, and it was like watching a sped-up clip of millions of ants rushing here and there at breakneck speed. Life is much slower in eternity.

I started trying to describe the experience to Frank, but he told me: 'Just breathe!'

A couple of weeks later, he mentioned that he'd been suffering from debilitating pain in his spine (around his kidneys) for some time before I had taken the ketamine. But on that night and while I was on it, the pain disappeared and hadn't returned since.

'Wow!' I blurted out and immediately started telling him about the way I had mended his spine . . . but he walked out of the room before the story really got going.

His message was that the ego (or personality) needs to share such stories, but that to invest energy in that level of reality was missing the point, which was to be in the transcendent state in the midst of the illusion. And the way to maintain that was through breathing.

Further explorations expanded my understanding of the archetypal level of reality. On one trip I would be hanging with the Greek gods, or at least seeing reality through their eyes; on another, I would be with travellers from a different solar system far away on the 'other side' of the galaxy, experiencing the speed of rushing through the outer reaches of space in order for me to see the curve of the universe.

Eventually, I had all the proof I needed that the Taoist methods I'd been studying – which I was using while on any of the drugs – were indeed valid. At that point, I made a clear decision to stop the sessions.

KARMIC INVESTIGATIONS

The discussion of the meaning of karma, meanwhile, was a constant. Frank had a natural grasp of it, along with an innate reticence to discuss it other than by inference. 'He who knows does not speak. He who speaks does not know', to quote Lao-tzu. I found, as with most of the great teachers, that the way to get them to throw light on a subject was by asking indirect questions.

One day I went to him and asked, 'Frank, do you think that at my stage of spiritual evolution, if I were to have an affair with a married woman, it would be bad karma?' I'd met someone recently who happened to be married, but with whom there was evidently huge chemistry. I was grappling with the pros and cons of it in my head.

He remained silent, sitting like a guru on his bed for quite a while, then turned to me slowly and said, 'How do you know it wouldn't be bad karma not to?'

In other words, who are we to presume to understand karma? Who are we to presume to understand right or wrong? And who are we to presume that we can see enough of the big picture, across lifetimes, in order to make any sort of valid judgments?

I chose not to get involved with the woman, incidentally. Then, as now, I followed my energy rather than any assumed set of morals, trusting that my inner wisdom would always lead me in the right direction; and it had led me away from her. (I'm tempted to go into that more, but it would bring me seductively close to talking about my whole take on sexuality and how I've conducted myself in that respect over the decades, through what has been a most unusual series of adventures. But I'll leave that for the autobiography, as it's not appropriate to this story.)

The gift Frank gave me was his honesty. He didn't play the game of pretence, which is the normal social currency. He played the game of realness, more so than anyone I'd met previously or have met since.

I'm still learning how to bring the real to the unreal world of the media, the milieu in which one way or another I make my living – hence how you come to have this book in your hands. It's not an easy task, and I understand more every day why Frank chose not to engage in it, even though what he had to teach was probably more valid and potentially useful to the world than any other teacher past or present, including even me.

From me, you get the palatable, generous, relatively soft version. Frank's style would have probably shaken the world up a tad too much for comfort. Where others are dealing with fearfulness and learning how to override it enough to function effectively, Frank was merely dealing with existential ennui. He had no fear. He had faced death in a hundred different ways and had no fear of it. In fact, he craved it because he knew he preferred the eternal state to the everyday realm. To the uninitiated, this might have been diagnosed as severe depression, but to those who knew him, it was clearly a result of absolute enlightenment and unprecedented warrior-like courage.

Either way it's just a view.

One day I found myself pacing up and down, grappling with some dilemma or other, and noticed that I was holding my breath. I heard Frank's voice – 'Breathe!' – and exhaled deeply. Suddenly, after all those years of him telling me to breathe, it finally hit me. Oh, yes! Breathe. I get it. Breathe!

It's amazing when something so simple yet so huge has been staring you in the face for so long and you haven't seen it, and then in an instant you see it and it changes your whole life just like everyone told you it would. It goes from being theoretical to real. That was Frank's gift to me. Through a variety of means and with the help of various chemical 'psycholaxatives' when necessary, he made the theoretical real for me.

Eventually, having managed to keep him interested in life for 12 years, and having got him embroiled in a hundred different creative projects of all sorts, I finally ran out of ideas. Ironically, for the one who taught me how to breathe (and who changed my life so profoundly in all senses through it), he taped a plastic bag over his head one day and suffocated himself. But then he was a master of irony.

He promised that he'd stay in touch when he was dead.

A few years before he died, I'd moved some stuff to my parents' attic, including a plaid laundry bag with lots of old clothes in it, which remained there untouched.

I used to lend Frank a pair of hair clippers. He'd borrowed them just before he'd died and hadn't returned them.

A couple of weeks after his death, I happened to go and collect the stuff at my parents' house. When I got it home, I found myself talking to Frank about staying in touch. I could feel him there, but I was saying that it could all just be my imagination.

Then Frank spoke. 'Have a look in the laundry bag – right at the bottom.'

So I stuck my hand in.

'Further – at the bottom,' he said. And there were the clippers.

I once asked him (when he was still alive), whether he reckoned my tendency to be a bit outrageous in the way I present myself and my material, and the way I live my life in general, would be an impediment to successfully getting the message out as far and wide as I believed it should go. Again a silence, then: 'You won't fail for being too outrageous. You may fail for not being outrageous enough, however.'

Frank taught me to be myself – dark and light, both and neither. He taught me to transcend preferences and to see life as theatre. He taught me to care less about the opinions of others and to care even less about my own opinions. He taught me that reality as we know it is merely a paradigm comprising a particular set of collective opinions. And he taught me to breathe. Perhaps there simply wasn't enough air in the world for both of us. I believe that was somehow the case, and he was perhaps one of the most generous people ever to live by giving me his quota.

INNER GURU

If I come from the view that at the deepest level I have created my reality – including having drawn all my teachers to me at the appropriate time and manner – I must also concede that every one of them was an external manifestation of my own internal guru in all his different guises, so to him, or her, must go my ultimate thanks and recognition. My path has been my path, and that aspect of it that led to me being The Barefoot Doctor would have been informed by the relevant teachings one way or the other, and the teacher would have appeared in one guise or another, depending on which actors were available to play the role at the time. But I have to say the particular actors that the Tao cast for the role were especially splendid and extraordinary, and I regularly pray that I'm doing them at least 10 per cent of the justice they deserve, in the way I translate their input to me for the world at large. If so, I'm doing a good job.

I'm a colourful character, of that there's no doubt. Compared to some of my teachers, however, I'm distinctly pastel-shaded. Perhaps the Tao knew that even this shading was about as much as the world would comfortably handle at this time, and so condensed all the wisdom of these incredible people and shunted it through me as the channel. At least that's how it feels.

I've been privileged, it's true, but I hope you've found this ramshackle account inspiring. It's no easy ride being a maverick; you bang up against the static element of society at every turn. But the rewards are the wealth of colours and flavours. I hope your mind feels more colourful and pleasantly flavoured for reading this.

I also hope that it encourages you to tune in to your own inner guru: the guiding voice that instructs you every step of the way, sometimes acted out for you in the guise of actual teachers who come along, sometimes just within you on the inner planes. For by following that voice you will be led on the most unimaginable adventures.

The journey is not always comfortable and is certainly not for those who only seek comfort. But it does feel like the ultimate act of worship, this willingness to surrender to the pull of the path.

*** ***

On 21st August, 1989, I was doing an acupuncture treatment on Neil Spencer, who used to be a rock critic. At the time, I'd always work barefoot, as it was more comfortable and less sweaty than wearing trainers all day. On my bookshelf was a copy of *A Barefoot Doctor's Manual*, the official publication the Chinese government put out every four years with all the latest techniques used by barefoot doctors.

I was looking for a name for my band and was brainstorming my ideas with Neil.

We went through a few, then I looked at the book and down at my naked feet and said, 'How about The Barefoot Doctor?'

And that was it. The Barefoot Doctor was born.

And for all the ridiculously juicy, riveting and fairly unbelievable adventures 'his' birth has brought to my life (which have continued growing in scale and scope ever since), please stand by for the autobiography, which I promise to write as soon as I get a really solid punch line.

*** ***

To download free videos of the exercises from the masters who taught me how to supercharge my life so that you can supercharge yours, go to www.superchargedtaoist.com now!

— The Barefoot Doctor

*** ***

About the Author

The Barefoot Doctor has been at the helm of the personal development movement in the United Kingdom for more than two decades. The author of 13 best-selling books, he has devoted his life to interpreting, simplifying and sharing the ancient Taoist system of medicine, martial arts, meditation and creativity. The Barefoot Doctor has a following of millions around the globe, who log on to his Website daily and attend his various talks, seminars, events and club nights.

Website: www.barefootdoctorglobal.com

*** ***

Notes

Notes

Notes

Notes

Notes

Hay House Titles of Related Interest

YOU CAN HEAL YOUR LIFE, the movie,
starring Louise L. Hay & Friends
(available as a 1-DVD programme and an expanded 2-DVD set)
Watch the trailer at: www.LouiseHayMovie.com

THE SHIFT, the movie,
starring Dr. Wayne W. Dyer
(available as a 1-DVD programme and an expanded 2-DVD set)
Watch the trailer at: www.DyerMovie.com

✳✳✳ ✳✳✳

Change Your Thoughts—Change Your Life:
Living the Wisdom of the Tao, by Dr. Wayne W. Dyer

The Compassionate Samurai: Being Extraordinary in an Ordinary
World, by Brian Klemmer

How Long Is Now? How to Be Spiritually Awake in the Real World,
by Tim Freke

Mirrors of Time: Using Regression for Physical, Emotional, and
Spiritual Healing (book with CD), by Brian L. Weiss, MD

F**k It: The Ultimate Spiritual Way, by John C. Parkin

The Reconnection: Heal Others, Heal Yourself, by Dr. Eric Pearl

Return to The Sacred: Ancient Pathways to Spiritual Awakening, by
Jonathan H. Ellerby, PhD

The 7 Secrets of Sound Healing (book with CD), by Jonathan Goldman

What Happens When We Die: A Groundbreaking Study into the
Nature of Life and Death, by Sam Parnia, MD

Yoga, Power, and Spirit: Patanjali the Shaman, by Alberto Villodo, PhD

All of the above are available at your local bookstore,
or may be ordered by contacting Hay House (see last page).

We hope you enjoyed this Hay House book.
If you would like to receive a free catalogue featuring additional
Hay House books and products, or if you would like information
about the Hay Foundation, please contact:

Hay House UK Ltd
292B Kensal Road • London W10 5BE
Tel: (44) 20 8962 1230; Fax: (44) 20 8962 1239
www.hayhouse.co.uk

***

Published and distributed in the United States of America by:
Hay House, Inc. • PO Box 5100 • Carlsbad, CA 92018-5100
Tel: (1) 760 431 7695 or (1) 800 654 5126;
Fax: (1) 760 431 6948 or (1) 800 650 5115
www.hayhouse.com

***

Published and distributed in Australia by:
Hay House Australia Ltd • 18/36 Ralph Street • Alexandria, NSW 2015
Tel: (61) 2 9669 4299, Fax: (61) 2 9669 4144
www.hayhouse.com.au

***

Published and distributed in the Republic of South Africa by:
Hay House SA (Pty) Ltd • PO Box 990 • Witkoppen 2068
Tel/Fax: (27) 11 467 8904
www.hayhouse.co.za

***

Published and distributed in India by:
Hay House Publishers India • Muskaan Complex • Plot No.3
B-2• Vasant Kunj • New Delhi - 110 070
Tel: (91) 11 41761620; Fax: (91) 11 41761630
www.hayhouse.co.in

***

Distributed in Canada by:
Raincoast • 9050 Shaughnessy St • Vancouver, BC V6P 6E5
Tel: (1) 604 323 7100
Fax: (1) 604 323 2600

***

Sign up via the Hay House UK website to receive the Hay House
online newsletter and stay informed about what's going on with your
favourite authors. You'll receive bimonthly announcements
about discounts and offers, special events, product highlights,
free excerpts, giveaways, and more!
www.hayhouse.co.uk